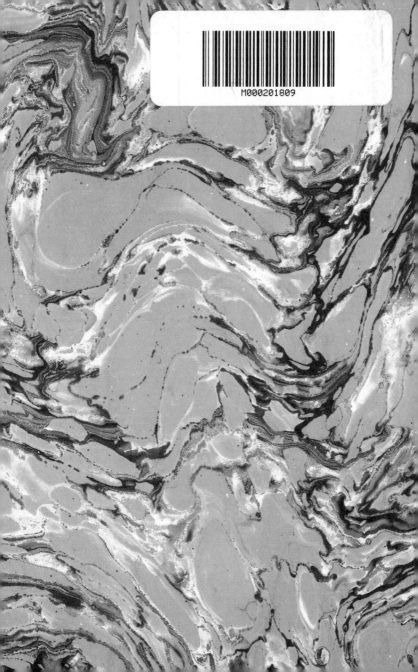

Sounds of the Morning Sun

Sounds of the Morning Sun

Diane Victoria Cirincione

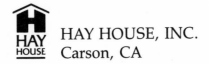
HAY HOUSE, INC.
Carson, CA

SOUNDS OF THE MORNING SUN
by Diane V. Cirincione

Copyright © 1993 by Diane Victoria Cirincione

Library of Congress Cataloging-in-Publication Data

Cirincione, Diane V.
    Sounds of the morning sun / Diane Victoria Cirincione.
        p.   cm.
    ISBN 1–56170–073–8 : $15.00
    1. Meditations.   I. Title.
BL624.2.C57   1993   93–33200
291.4'3—dc20   CIP

Library of Congress Catalog Card No. 93–33200
ISBN: 1–56170–073–8

Jacket Design and Painting by Robert Hunt
Typesetting by Freedmen's Organization, Los Angeles, CA 90004

93 94 95 96 97 98   10 9 8 7 6 5 4 3 2 1
First Printing, October 1993

Published and Distributed in the United States by:

Hay House, Inc.
P.O. Box 6204
Carson, CA 90749–6204

Printed in the United States of America

Dedication

Sounds of the Morning Sun is dedicated to those who have broken from the trauma of everyday living; to those who have gathered the will to survive and go on; to those who have faced their shadow and are able to see its relationship to their sun; to those who have the courage to open their wounds and to heal; and to those who have the vision to see their own transformation as a microcosm of the world.

Acknowledgments

This book has evolved over many years and through certain periods of my own transformational process. Those who have touched my life have included the thousands of individuals in my lectures and workshops this past decade who have had the courage to be vulnerable in order to heal. As they, one by one, opened their closets to let the skeletons out, my skeletons walked out too, only to find them, years later, as angels in disguise. I may not remember all of your names, but your stories have reached my hidden places and touched me in a way that I will always remember.

Very special recognition to my spouse, and partner in life, Jerry Jampolsky, whose love has truly become unconditional. I thank him for his undaunting encouragement and support to complete and publish this work.

To my family, both biological and extended, I express my continued, deep appreciation for each and every one of you for the nurturing, friendship, and guidance you have so generously given me.

For inspiration and the courage to change, I thank my mother, Filomena Biele Girard. Her faith and vulnerability, her optimism and curiosity along with her undying support continue to bless my life.

Those precious friendships in my life know who they are and what they mean to me. Even though the years and some circumstances may have changed, each continues to hold a unique place in my heart for what we have shared with and learned from each other.

Boundless thanks to my dear friend, Betty Karr, whose tender, loving care of both the manuscript and the author was a mainstay of support for this work.

Much appreciation to Reid Tracy and the folks at Hay House for their faith in this book. Special gratitude to Dan Olmos and his support staff for making it all so easy.

Special appreciation goes to artist/illustrator, Robert Hunt, for his original work and input on the cover design.

Also to Susan Oristaglio for her outstanding photographic contribution.

Finally, I would like to thank the staff, the volunteers, and participants at the Center for Attitudinal Healing in Tiburon, California for all they have taught me about learning to live and learning to die, about loving and letting go, and about teaching what I want to learn.

Contents

PART TWO

The Search for Self

PART THREE

The Journey Home

Introduction

Sounds of the Morning Sun is a personal journey of the evolution of consciousness of a single soul. Here unfolds the tug of war, the struggle of the ego as defined in self-determined goals which confronts head-on the emergence of awakening consciousness.

The journey I attempt to take within these pages is the longest journey in the world. It is the hardest, perhaps the most foreign, and surely the most frightening. It is also, however, the ultimate and inevitable journey that we each will travel in order to find our way Home. It is truly the longest journey in the world, yet only a few inches, as we travel out of our heads and into our hearts. It is a search for Peace, a search for Love and a beginning of the search for Self.

This work is an expression of freedom in the choice to explore the incredible mystery of the Divine through personal journeying, rather than someone else's limited description or dictated path.

It is the choice to no longer relinquish the search for the spiritual Self to an organization, institution, or theological subscription, but to respect the ability of each of us to access any of these if, or when, appropriate as catalysts for spiritual growth.

It is a decision to cleanse the limited, polarized perception of a male-favored or male-dictated spirituality from my reality, replacing it with the inherently abundant duality of the feminine Goddess and the masculine God.

Spiritual accessibility to the Source is neither ordained nor ministered, but is a grace bestowed upon all of us born to this earth by that which created it. The cultural, nationalistic, religious, racial, or gender differences I have observed throughout the world are not capable of severing our universal connections to the Source. Rather, it is only personal belief systems proliferated throughout the ages that give the perception that one religious path homeward is more correct than others, intimating that one is "right," so the others must be somehow "wrong." I cannot help but believe that when we sincerely put in a call to God, it doesn't matter what telephone booth we use to make the call. All of them are going to get there and all calls will be answered.

During the many years in which this work unfolded, over thirty descriptive words naming that which is the Source of all life emerged to express the boundless universality of that which is not comprehensible within the limitations of the human mind.

Spirit, the Light, Creator, Mother Father God, Infinite Power, Home, Morning Light, the Presence are but a few of the ways I found comfortable to express that which is inexpressible. All other references to a Higher Power are capitalized throughout including the direct expression of ''You.'' The reference to someone else other than Spirit throughout these pages is to my beloved spouse, friend and partner, Jerry Jampolsky. It is in the spirit of our ongoing efforts to create a truly holy and equal relationship that I share some of the challenges of our relationship and the resulting awarenesses with you for each intertwines with the personal relationship with God.

The sun drenched morning light of November 13, 1979 provided the experience of a reawakened reunion between my Higher Self and personality self. Totally blinded by the overwhelming brilliance of the early morning sun rising above Angel Island, my consciousness filled with words, streaming, two and three at a time. Although they seemed to make sense, I was nevertheless compelled to write them down in order to release the space as more immediately followed. Only at the end of a seemingly timeless thirty minutes or so would I dare to read them in their connected pattern of structured sentences. That first morning it flowed as a single thought and ended with:

"Don't be afraid to listen to the sounds of the morning sun. It brings with it each day the source of physical life and the symbolism of our Eternal One. Let your way be lighted and warmed by its golden rays and quiet strength, perfectly harmonious with us, yet so distant. Listen to the sounds of the morning sun as it enlightens your day and the way to Peace. Let your Inner Self speak, finally introducing you to Yourself. Be confident, not afraid. You will love the Self you hear with total trust. Begin to be and we will finally be One again."

I sit here often in the sun's first light as the early morning hours feed into days and the months meander into years. The words drift and flow as they lay gently on my mind. Thoughts are not formulated or preconceived in any manner familiar to me within the realm of my ordinary senses. Beyond these five points of reference and any conscious plan the questions arise, possibilities ponder, ideas flow, and answers appear as if from some distant point of view. Yet, I know all too well that they come from within the inner planes of my Being; the "me" that has been before and will continue on beyond the shadows of the illusion of death. Undeniable is the cry of the personality self longing to reunite with the Higher Self, a soul integration.

The sun, the source of our physical life and the

symbolism of our Eternal One, is used as a metaphor for the Light of spiritual enlightenment throughout the internal moments of these writings, as I look to nature in the form of the seasons, the rains, the wind, the sea, the moon and beyond for parallel lessons to help differentiate what is real, what is lasting and what is true.

In Part I, *''Sounds of the Morning Sun,''* many questions arose and answers followed as nature was revealed as a map to the answers to many questions and Love was viewed as the ultimate path homeward. Home is seen as the place of all beginnings and endings where God dwells, the Great Spirit and Source of Creation of all life.

It all seemed so clear and simple until the challenge of application dimmed my light and the battle was waged between the illusion of ego and the reality of Spirit. Part II, *''The Search For Self,''* begins with agony and turmoil, dashing hopes of a ''quick enlightenment'' in the answer:

''It is now that I must remember that the small and seemingly insignificant deeds of each day appear to have little value; yet, they are like layer upon layer of feathers that make up magnificent wings; each has value and each an important place in making up the whole.'' . . . ''The daily acts of learning to live and love and share and accept will be my food for enlightenment. I will feign distractions and be tolerant of myself. I have chosen this way and will not fight what I know in my heart to be right.''

''*The Journey Home*,'' Part III, questions the physical, emotional as well as spiritual path; a journey directed no longer from the head but from deep within the heart, from soul consciousness. What had become clear is that the mental altar at which I had worshipped for so many years was no longer a sanctuary. The turmoil and inconsistencies, the resistance and ultimate triumphs became my havens along the way on my journey back home to the Source.

I am not a writer by either ambition or design. I only know that somewhere I have given ''permission'' for this integrated flow to occur, charting in full consciousness the evolution of an individual soul. ''She'' is me, yet ''she'' is also you for we are one and the same only in another frame of reference. I offer her to you as part of yourself as we travel together through the dark corridors of the mind in search of the Light.

PART ONE

Sounds of the Morning Sun

Sounds of the Morning Sun

The miracle of night blending into day . . .
Light is a gift. The sun is liken to Enlightenment. Always there, ever present, ever emerging to brighten our way from the darkness of night and our minds.

We take for granted both the light from the day and our Inner Light. We must come to recognize their magnificent Source.

The balance in nature is perfect as is our connection with Oneness. We can learn again the simple perfection which is natural to us and the planet around us.

Don't be afraid to listen to the sounds of the morning sun. It brings with it each day the source of our physical life and the symbolism of our eternal one. Let your way be lighted and warmed by its golden rays and quiet strength, perfectly harmonious with us, yet so distant.

Listen to the sounds of the morning sun as it enlightens your day and the way to peace. Let your Inner Self speak, finally introducing you to yourself.

Be confident, not afraid. You will love the Self you hear with total trust. Begin to be and we will finally be one again.

Greeting the Enlightenment

When humankind realizes its oneness, its connection beyond life, there will be true peace and mutual growth in love and respect for our differences. They are indeed so very small when we recognize the bond that binds us together as part of the One Universe.

Come. Let us join as the children at play and the creatures of the earth. Let us join at greeting the Enlightenment as it comes again in our time and space. Let us each prepare for the coming of Light, an end to loneliness, the coming of Love.

Open our hearts and minds and spirits to the enrichment we can learn from the living creatures and plants around us.

Share. Accept. Love one another, and nature and all things natural will abound.

Hope of the Rising Sun

Hope of the rising sun. It will rise, but will I be aware to greet it and accept its message?

Enlightenment will come. It will attempt to rise in my Inner Self. Will I know it? Will I be aware of its life form? Or will another life pass in darkness and ignorance, paving the steps with greed and ambition; wasting precious years on misguided, superficial paths?

Learn from the small creatures of the earth. They are in harmony with nature and at peace. I must achieve this first in order to rise to the next plane, one of spiritual enlightenment and unlimited growth; a time when the gentleness of the conscious mind will blend as one with the Inner Spirit.

Expectations

The rising sun holds great expectations. Will it bless us another day with its bounty of warmth? The creatures, the plants, and I await its decision. Ah yes. Constant love, consistent warmth, day after day, it never disappoints us.

If I look to the Light it will always be there, never changing, ever constant; only my awareness grows with each rotation.

Open my eyes to see the Light; open my body to feel it; and open my inner heart to experience its glow.

Love one another and we will bask in its Golden Rays for eternity together.

The Search

My search must be for the whole enlightenment. I cannot bask in its rays, involve my ego in its abilities, or discuss its truths if I do not seek to embody the whole concept of the natural connection between nature and humankind.

I will be silent until there is part of the original Light to share with others and will not strive to impress with particles of others thoughts. I will wait—watch—be patient for my own offerings.

The Light shines each day, shedding its warmth and truth. Turn to face it; to really see what it offers me. I must seek its awareness or days will follow months and the years will pass as I blindly forge through the rubble I have created as barriers to the Truth. As these bypasses are recognized and set aside, the way is made for recognizing my true reality. I can achieve enlightenment as I allow my petals to unfold in its generous warmth and energy.

Illusions

False illusions drain my creative energies and these transparent goals divert me from the one pursuit towards illusive gains. As I take toll in the stock I possess mentally, physically, emotionally, and spiritually, and weigh it on the scales of life, I find the balance is imperfect because my pursuits are shallow, limited, transparent and illusive. Until I recognize why I am here and what I am meant to achieve, I will wander in self-doubt, disillusionment, and sadness.

I am joyful at the expectation of discovering the Light. There are many to help me if I just ask and be open to their guideposts along the way.

Lessons

Isn't it a joy to grow wiser each day and hope that all lessons learned are remembered and the signposts along the way read? Even though I oftentimes forget and must experience again the pain of learning, and even though my vision gets foggy and the messages are sometimes unclear, let me celebrate each day my freedom of choice. Going forward each step is fulfilling, but let me not be too harsh on myself when the step is occasionally backwards. My heart becomes heavy when my daily distractions are taken too seriously. Are any of them really that important when I consider the overall Plan?

I must strive to discover the basic meanings of why I am here and what I am to accomplish in this short time.

The blossoming bud can only bloom if all its surroundings are balanced; the soil; the sun; and the rest of nature. If I try to balance my life away from extremes towards a harmonious, quiet peace, I will discover the simplistic beauty in my natural surroundings. I blend naturally with this and unnaturally with the concrete world that has been created.

I look to the morning sun for a symbol of life, vision, warmth, and consistent support.

Friendship

Friendship is a part of nature. It is based on natural love and not the superficial accessories we surround ourselves with, for they have no real value at all. Let us grow together. And when our skin wrinkles and our pace hesitates, if our eyes fade or our minds forget, that will be alright too. For these visions and strengths are only physical and not of any lasting importance. We will be blessed with real vision and unlimited strength if we only listen to our Inner Self. All of the answers are there if we are wise enough to ask and quiet enough to hear. Let us work together for this brief time to hear our True Voice and experience a moment of real peace.

Harmony

Harmony is the highest order of things and is found in the balance between nature and humans. It is to be encouraged, respected, and preserved.

Peace in the world arises from the respect between humans and the smallest insect. Each has a right to the planet and each must inherit its state.

City Dwellers

Ah, city dwellers, rise to the morning sun. You receive it first in your high concrete vaults. How lucky you are. A tunnel of light breaks the dawn. Receive it with joy and excited anticipation of what wisdom will come.

Morning Light, star bursts into day, Your glow begins to warm our concrete, plastic world. Even in our boxes You spread Nature's glow all around us. You still bear with us. Is it tolerance You show? No, it is joy at our efforts. You love us beyond what we are here. How much love You must have.

Morning Glow

Morning Glow, raise us to the level where we might be. Shed Your rays of hope and love and peace on our darkened minds and free our spirits to soar as the birds do. Oh Great Spirit, journey with me to catch the Light of the Morning Sun. Raise me in the sky so I might glimpse at its magnificence.

It loves us, each and every one of the creatures of the earth. Totally accepting and continuously embracing; love never ending, always renewing our tested spirits.

Let us join together in love and peace under the one Light that embraces us all. We are the child crying in the cold night. Love embraces us with its Source of Life, always constant, never ending. The gift is here every morning. Receive it with the understanding that tomorrow will also be a lighted path. Never despair that you are alone, for that state does not exist.

The Light is always around us—always there if we only look up to see its glow. Be joyful at the expectations of the new day inside each of us. Be silent and receive its abundance. It's Light is the only thing that is real. The rest is illusion and distraction.

Look to the Morning Sun and reach for its Light. Hold it in your heart for as long as you are; and whenever you can, turn to share its warmth with the other creatures, for they may be in a shadow and the only Source will be your Light. Share, love and be at peace.

Flight

How balanced the beauty of nature. Behold its magnificence in the birds in the air. The morning rays warm their wings and the light beckons them to soar to new heights.

Morning Light, warm my wings and energize my flight to new heights of love and awareness. You are the Source of all light and love and hope. Guide me and protect me from the darkness. Help me rise from the deep of night with Your blanket of warmth and understanding. You know it is alright for me to fall; but I, each day, am cross with the anxieties of failure. Teach me Your patience and be my example of understanding and tolerance for my fellow beings.

We all try so very hard to seek the Light and when we fall, as we often do, You are there to soften the fall and ease the hurt. If we only accept and recognize that You are there right by our side all of the time, our short stay here would be more joyful and tolerant. Teach us not only love and acceptance of the differences in those around us, but open us to accept ourselves as part of You. Oh gift of the Morning Sun—

I accept You with open heart and a humble but loving spirit to learn Your way—the path to peace and happiness beyond this brief journey into the next.

Spirit, soar to the mountain top to greet your friend the sun. Let it know that although we do not always see, or hear, or feel its warmth and love, we still need the fundamental promise of continuity; one that will carry us from our darkened night to the promise of each new day.

Braids of Gold

Let us gather in the light of morning to give praise for the gift that is ours.

Morning clouds fired with Your Light streak the sky like braids of gold.

I await You with patience and confidence that You will come to warm the new day with light and love. Let me reflect Your Glow even in my bleakest hours for You are strength for us all, creatures large and small.

Morning Glow, rise into day and strike Your Light of Knowledge to the darkest places of my mind. Enlighten my heavy, preoccupied existence with words of the way to unity. Lest I feel alone, show me the cord that binds us together as creatures deserving to inherit the Universe.

Love binds us all. It lightens the darkened night in my heart and allows my Inner Glow to shine for my fellow beings. I will share the Light I have been given for that is the only way it will grow stronger, this bond of love and caring that binds us.

Let those floundering in the night of their days bask

in Your warmth and Light; and then, they too, will someday come to the awareness that we are all part of the Universal One. The only way it is kindled is by opening my heart to share it, thus intensifying its force.

Morning clouds cover Your rays like the distractions of our daily lives. Let me work to pass through these clouds; and, while I recognize their reality, let me lay claim only to the one reality which they hide.

Morning Light, begin to teach me the gift of love and living. Encourage me to share the gifts You so readily pass to me. I know that You love me. My ignorance is on what level You have chosen to communicate? Guide me to openness for truth and honesty in learning to love You in return.

I now know that this must be done through those around me. If they cannot see You at first, they may be able to glimpse at Your Light through me. Share the Way of Light with me, so that I may journey towards You; and in doing so lead my fellow beings.

Enlighten my path in order that I may be worthy to walk Your way. Love me forever with the only reality I really know.

No Reflections, No Illusions

No reflections, no illusions. The Light becomes day awakening me with its illumination as I rise to conquer the darkness of night. Fill me with Your Rays to overcome the darkness in my mind. Enlighten my heart to the possibilities of Your love. Darkened and shadowed places fill with Your beams of Light as Your bounty flows freely.

I open the dark places of my heart and spirit so that You may enter freely. Come and fill me that I might bask in Your warmth and Light and love. Fill me to the brim in order that others may see Your Rays emitting from me. Let them see and share my Light if You are indeed shadowed from them as I glow with the fire of Eternal Life.

Teach me to recognize the love around me and guide me to pass it on to others. Love is meant to share for it is the cure for our bruised existences. Help me to mend other's wounded hearts and heal them with lasting peace.

Teach me friend, Morning Light, the simplistic way to inner harmony and compatibility with You. Focus my vision and let me not be distracted by the lower levels of development. Spirit, help me soar with swift speed to greet the physical light each morning and to see the spiritual Light each day in my fellow beings.

I yearn for Peace. How come it aches so when I look at what we have done?

Reflections on the Dew

Morning light, reflecting on the dew a million images of the sun. So, too, are the number of ways in which we can see and find our path home.

No one way is wiser or better than the other. Since we differ, we are provided with the choice to select that which is best for us. The differences are beautiful for in time they all lead us Home.

Teach us not to grovel in the confusion of how we are not the same. Each being's path is precious to them. We must learn not only tolerance of other's ways that are different from our own, but actually come to love the customs and dreams that have separated us in the past.

Who knows, for if our path is not the most gratifying, we might come to look to theirs to seek understanding. As we open our hearts and minds to the beauty of the differences we will come to know our own way.

The Journey Inward

Day breaks, the light comes, the birds fly as the mist rises. My bus-i-nesses begin again. I toil with intolerance at daily tasks, floundering in a sea of confusion, doubt, and self-delusion. My roles dominate the patterns of my daily life. Succeed, project, reflect, proceed. Where am I going and for whom and why?

Morning dawn breaks into day. The light has come once again. Do I still live in the shadowy existence of my exterior self, immersed in my numerous distractions? How simple my journey would be if I could come to understand that the Light comes only from within, not amidst the exterior shadows. The final road is enriched with signposts leading the way to a loving reality. I must journey inward.

The Guiding Light

Your morning glow tints the dawn with rays of golden warmth as the birds fly to greet you.

Good morning, good morning! Oh, how I have missed You these mist-filled days.

Your beams reach out to each blade of grass. The mountains' crest frames your image, portrait of life. The morning sky embraces and gently brings you forth.

Why do I think of the Light most when you are gone from me? Why is your absence more important than your presence which I so recklessly take for granted? I want you there so I may draw from you only when I am in need. How desperate my attempts to grab hold of you to bring my feeble plays together.

As I learn to look towards the Light, I can then accept guidance and love all of the days of my life. Your abundance is one which flows freely with a dependent continuity. Yet, I only drink from Your waters when I am desperately thirsty.

Teach me to accept Your offerings each day. Then

I will gather strength and confidence to love others in return with the continuity they deserve.

My daily desperations dominate and distract my energies away from any meaningful purpose. Following Your Guiding Light will lead me to the fountain. Free me to drink from Your waters of love and enlightenment so I may glow with Your Light. Open my heart and mind and body to Your glow in order that it may shine through me to others.

Your smallest insect is as important as each of us in this chain of love. When I can come to realize its value and right to life, then I will begin to see real equality.

Morning Light, let me travel inward on Your Golden Rays which warm my being. Nourish me in order that I might flower. I know many will try to hide or even destroy the beauty there. Give me strength to continue to grow and guide me to bear the news You would send forth through me.

I want so to come home. Help me to do my best as Your guide for others to see. Please take care of me for I am often frightened amidst the turmoils of individuals and their pursuits. I ask Your protection so that I may continue to learn and teach in return.

Humble me to the place where I will best function to fulfill my purpose. Remove the distractions and worries from my path in order that I might begin the journey homeward and return to You with speed.

The Sabbath

O h, good morning on this Your day; one which we have set aside to proclaim Your existence. How foolish we are to bottle You on a shelf for the rest of Your days and only sing You to glory on the Sabbath.

We are the losers who distract ourselves with consumption and goal making all the rest of the time, rarely stopping to seek or recognize Your omnipresent glory in the smallest of flowers or the kindest of deeds. We see You only when we are in need, seeking a crutch.

Prejudice and fear fill our motivations. Even Your houses of worship are pitted against each other, consumed with self-righteous ideologies; even Your very name is argued upon. How sad that we all recognize Your Presence, but we are not capable of accepting Your Universality.

Your Light shines through so many barriers, beyond even the dark prejudices of our minds if we only open the door and ask to see You.

Teach me the patience and understanding necessary to see You as others do for their vision holds other dimensions of Your love which possibly my perspective cannot view. There is so much each of us has to give and share in our descriptions of You. How desperately we hold to our own few taught fragments of reality when Your true Light can be seen through a composite of all the loving truths evolved through our diversified beliefs, customs and traditions.

We are multiples of a puzzle fighting to stay apart; yet, images of You can only be seen when we each offer our part, freely and unafraid, to make the whole a mirror of You. Only then, when we accept all other differences and ways to the Light as equal to our own, can we truly walk on the path homeward to You.

Be patient with us, dear Friend, and open our eyes to Your Morning Glow, the food for our long awaited journey. And even if we all cannot make the journey safely this time, help us share what we have obtained with others so that the next part of their trip will be just a little easier and more enlightened.

Teach us to love and share and accept those around us, for they are simply in another time of reference; all a part of the whole journeying to You and our place by Your side. Teach us to help those different from ourselves to our Light. Show them not the dark side of ourselves, but the image of You. Clear our vision to see in each and every one of Your creatures rays of Your warmth and love. It is there. We need only look.

Patience

Teach me the patience time will seed in my heart to accept the differences which separate others in direct conflict with me. Your Light is not to be used only when life is agreeable. Open my shadowed mind to accept Your teaching when it is hardest to envision love and acceptance (if not understanding) in another.

I fail so miserably when, while carrying Your words, I sink to the depths of personal motivations seeking revenge and justice. Teach me that love and true understanding are not part-time endeavors we mask ourselves in when all is well and when praise will be ours. True enlightenment places us all equally before You on the road homeward. Let me help to lift the barriers before others, not place them there or bolt them to the ground. I should see Your Light in others; yet, I have often failed to open my heart when anger and pride bind its seams tightly closed. Give me confidence to lay my heart open freely and willingly to others. And if in doing so, they periodically take from it and give nothing in return, let me remember the ''before'' when You always filled it again with

Your ever flowing and ever glowing love.

If I were only able to love myself and others as You do, so accepting and understanding of all our fears, desires, needs, and failures. How gentle and totally loving You are. My being fills with love for Your incredible capacity to love us now, before and after each fumbling day.

During the passages of time show me the way. Let me first learn to freely love myself as You do; to master my falls and sing glory to my successes; forward moving and always in reach of Your love.

Open my eyes and heart to see and accept Your generous and ever forgiving love for I am You and You are me. The only separation is in my mind isolating me from You and those around me.

Give me confidence to not be afraid of my own existence and survival. If I recognize my part of the Universal One, then the illusion of the possibility of failing alone will cease to exist.

Beauty

You make me smile, partially on my lips and deeply in my heart, when I see your perfection rise above the hills each morning.

What many faces have been borne to me in this Golden Age of the conscious mind. Their magnificent beauty is ever-changing.

Sometimes it is difficult if not impossible to recognize the Source in these other forms. We have stereotyped even You, Breaker of Dawn, Creator of all life.

The narrow channels of our minds bend and mold You to fit our images. It is no wonder we cannot see beyond these shallow mirages.

Your true excitement lies in the ever changing beauty of Your form. This I need to seek in the farthest corners of the earth, under the heaviest of rocks and in the saddest of hearts.

Beauty is not what we have prefabricated it to be, but what is unpackaged and natural. It is all that flows with the winds and the waters . . . life born free from the earth and man's seed into woman. These things are all Your magnificence in ever changing forms and impressions.

Teach me to awaken each day to the light of dawn in each aspect of my existence. Uncloud my mind from the distractions I create to fill the columns of days.

Time Eternal will hold all truths known for me to see. Pass my journey into the next with loving speed; yet while I am a dweller here in this place of my own description, open me to the world that surrounds me. You are here in all of Your splendor. How naive of me to think You had left me for this brief journey to make my way alone. You are here and there, in each leaf and in every heart. I smile once again not at Your joyful giving of love, but at myself for forgetting Your total encompassing of me.

Hold me close and calm my days to a level of serenity whereby I may begin to remember once more the "before." Your Light is so bright it blinds my vision once again awakening me to the reality that it is not with my eyes that I see You, nor my ears that I hear You, nor with my fingers that I touch You, for You are in me, one in the same, not a separate reality. Teach me again to remember Your Presence as totally encompassing and time-forever. You are the Guest in me and I invite You to guide my way Home.

The Presence

I did not plan to see you today for morning mist and heavy transient fog cover you from view. I was sure you would not be there. And, yet, as I turned to go, your face was perfectly clear and totally visible. Gone again, I see you only momentarily as the fog opens it's embrace. The moments the path is clear you are perfect in your circular form. This is the first I have seen you without your golden rays blinding my vision.

Why have you shown yourself to me so clearly? Is it only because I have taken the time to look for you in the morning sky?

Circular perfection and never ending continuity, protecting us from darkened days on a lifeless plane. You come and go and then again, yet I know you are always there. Do you tell me that our spiritual vision is often blocked by surface distractions liken to morning mist? Even though the Presence is always there, I need faith to believe and remember that reality. When it is gone from view, the dark side of my mind wanders and drifts on unchartered paths of distraction away from the Light and towards complex confusions.

The Light beckons in the distance even though it is not visible. Teach me to feel and recognize and follow the signposts during those moments when I cannot see.

Morning sun, you are magnificent in your brilliance. I am blinded by your light, yet I can finally see. We need not our eyes to see the Light. Bless both those with and without vision to look inward in search of the Guiding Light for it is only within that we will really begin to see and to be.

The Wings of Change

Change is all that really is on this plane. Nothing is completely still. The rotation of the planet is the basic premise for this reality as all answers are found parallel in what is natural. The change from light to dark and dark to light again offers to us each day the lesson change; yet, we rarely, if ever, see it as such.

The varying degrees of dawn and dusk reflect the natural variations which surround and encompass us. We cling to who we are or are yet to become, and to the persons and things that identify us as such. We work to make life happen in a certain way so as to ascertain specific reflections from ourselves and others. We clutch to what is here and now; we delve on what has been; and we work to control what will be to insure our identifications.

Think of the possibilities for freedom in allowing everything to pass with a detachment from its importance. What we then have is what would have occurred anyway, but with precious, all-encompassing energies not wasted on the inevitable. All will change except our identity and connection with the

Whole. That is everything that is real and constant. All else will come to pass.

The differences in us lie in the degrees of importance we place upon these things called our surroundings or environments. If we can but accept their beauty and metamorphosis, then peace will begin to be ours and change will be our choice as presented to us each moment. To be mindful of what is transpiring within opens the soul to experience all that which is around us without resistance, expectations, or programmed response.

We are designed to live together cohesively as part of a Whole. Perhaps the original plan was that all creatures, large and small, human and insect, would help to fulfill the balance, thereby creating an environment for growth and knowledge-seeking.

Why have the scales not balanced? Have we tipped them to pursue only our vain, superficial goals, seconding all others in our level of importance?

You filled us with love, curiosity, and a naive vulnerability when we entered this journey. Have our defenses for pursuit and survival forced us to subject creatures equal to us in order to gain control of our environment? And when the control is gained, what has been the result? Waste and pollution, starvation and violence against this place we have called Your home.

If we can kill another seeker, are we no less violent

to destroy our natural surroundings? Is polluting a river any less wanton than polluting a young mind? Our values have been warped and twisted to fit our momentary or cultural needs, moulding even our image of You to support our goals and pursuits.

Respect, the necessary ingredient in our food for growth, must be recognized, nurtured, and made a part of our daily diet. Respect oftentimes comes with understanding, yet it is not realistic that we can understand all during one of our journeys here. We must, therefore, offer this aspect, this respect, even when we do not fully agree or understand.

All ways are not our ways and we should neither expect or try to cause them to be. The Whole cannot function if all are the same, for what would be the point if all paths were equal and laid before us? What would we learn or accomplish on our journey? No, it is the differences that make all creatures so very special and important in the overall plan. Even though we find these differences the hardest to deal with at times, teach us their great value and guide us away from efforts to crush these opposites with our fearful bodies and protective minds.

If we can at some moment in time truly believe that Spirit loves us all, each creature large and small, then this belief will allow us to begin to build a foundation that will support all seekers in their journeys.

There are times when it seems impossible to understand the motives and rationale of others. During these moments, guide me to look towards the Light in order that I might gain a balance and if not understand, at least try to accept them. It is so difficult to consistently love when our own needs for survival arise. Clear my vision, especially at those moments, to see my spiritual capabilities for I can draw from them along the way. Teach me and guide me to remember the love the Spirit is when my mind is clouded and my vision blurred in anger or self-righteous indignation.

We all began as love and will return to love in full consciousness for in fact we have never left.

Distractions

Come to us, Morning Light. We so desperately need You to brighten our way. Rainbow aura, You reflect all that is natural here that You have created.

We come to You on different paths via different means. So diverse are our journeys that some cannot even be recognized as such. You draw us to You, Maker of Life, we who are barely capable of seeing You. Clouded by day and darkened by night, should the moon's reflection remind us that the light is still with us even when we cannot see the sun's magnificent brightness?

Overcast days and distracting goals of preoccupied time clutter our view of the Light. In time, we will come to realize Your Presence regardless of the climatic or personal coverups.

Weary journeyers on the path home, gather us together to support, not hinder, each others way.

Distractions clutter our thoughts so that even sleep holds no peace. Golden Light of day, clear our minds of superficial waste and make way for thoughts bringing peace and harmony. Questions are answered, all words are lasting and truthful. Reality will take hold and we will be clear forever to live in love and knowledge.

Time is deceiving as it carries from life to life lessons learned as we journey closer to home. Where am I now and from whence have I come? To You is where I will go. I now know that. Yet, I have already known Your Presence during this mandala of time for I could not yearn for You so if I already did not know.

Inner Light, glow and continue to bring Your abundance of knowledge to my conscious mind. Let me seek further Divinity here while I am still in the darkness of ignorance. I open my mind to what You have to teach me, You in me that has come so far on this journey in time. You seem so sure and so knowing. Give me the confidence to hear and accept Your knowingness of the Whole and what part I play in it.

Let me discover and recognize through You my importance to myself in order that other daily incidents will have less and less significance in my balance of daily existence. As I come to accept confidence, my purpose and part in the Whole will become clear and each task will have a true relationship with You.

The journey is sometimes long. Let me clear the way for the Lantern of Light You offer me illuminating the dark corners of my mind and heart.

Contemplation

Let me take just one moment to say hello to You today. Greetings, Giver of Life. You bless each day with Your Glow.

We are so often rushed and pushed awaiting the pressures of phones, buses, appointments, and goals. Quiet me. Soothe the anxieties I have created as fillers of days and mental spaces.

You bring quiet peace and harmony. If I cannot totally bask in Your gifts, then teach me to blend them with my tasks of earthly living. So desperate are the needs to survive in a fashionable way.

Monastic contemplation amidst the temple bells is not realistically compatible with the responsibilities for most who must provide for themselves and others.

During my moments of contemplation give me the words as tools for those trying to blend the two—enlightenment and survival. Many of us will come to know that survival is only a perimeter of our mental-making and that all is relative to our own thoughts.

Clear my mind of the debris I have laid there and help me to be free to claim the space as I see fit. I want

You to live there, and even though daily need will also make way, I want to embrace Your thoughts in order to integrate them into my daily actions.

There is a choice amongst us. Look with love and kindness upon us when we choose away from You in order to fulfill our own desperately important, momentary needs. Hold us close to You when we are weakest and are straying farthest.

For those of us who already know You, guide us to acknowledge clearly Your Light and to begin to share it with others through whatever gifts we possess, be it songs or words, acts or examples. Teach us the subtle, gentle persuasion of love in order that we may share Your peace with others.

Love is only real when it is in motion.

Daybreak

Your light shines in many ways and in many colors.

Daybreak into dawn, you appear separate from us at first, distant in the clouds. Having covered other lands, you now come to start our daily venture. Energies past spent on the exercise of goal-making. Exhausted and fading, we look inside to the shallow void. Accomplishments and success fill us with momentary food, nourishing only if our basic foundation is cultivated in Spirit, united with love of the Whole.

Daybreak into dawn, clear the way for a day filled with many aspects of life. Bless us with the ease to accomplish the tasks of our own making and let us not drain our energies so that we have nothing left to search for the Light.

I think I cannot see You and patiently wait for a glimpse of Your Light. I look to glance in a turn and You are there before me in Your splendid glory, not just Your Light but Your whole embodiment. Is it because I wanted to see? Because I waited in hopefulness? Because I chose to look for You that I saw? What of those who have no knowledge? How are they to recognize Your Presence? This recognition must come prior to acceptance. What of them? Are some to pass many times in darkness before they begin to see the Light? And of these can we be of no help? Who will see in this coming time of a new found consciousness?

It pains me to look at some now knowing that this encounter will not be the one for them. Should I then seek out those who are now becoming and those who have become aware of Your Presence?

We cannot do all for all. Teach me the gift of recognition in those moments of evaluation. Let me pass love and understanding to each of my fellow creatures, not excluding the smallest who live in the earth and sea and sky.

Many of us will find the road home in this life. Gather us to become aware of our bond together, our mutual pathways. Teach us only love and openness, for each vision varies. Help us to remember that sharing our signposts with others will only hasten new ones into view and speed our journey homeward to You and the Light.

Daybreak into dawn, Gift of Light, guide me to influence only in the good. Settle my ego on a blanket of Your peace so it will not block or distort the way. Take me, Your child, and soothe the pain while easing the hurt. Send me forth to share all that is open to me and to gather in return a new perspective of the mystery that is You.

Tolerance

Sunrise, when covered by clouds are you no less magnificent in your source? When darkened in doubt and confusion, are we no less a part of the Whole? Momentary changes of negative overcast shadow us only superficially. In reality we are still who we are, struggling to learn on our journey. You are never less and neither are we. Your patience and tolerance and love embody us during all actions and deeds regardless of how far reaching or backwards they may be.

As part of the Whole, we differ in that we lack the patience and tolerance needed to understand both ourselves and those we encounter. Once we can learn these qualities, we can begin to feel secure in our identification.

We flounder and fight and forge into other lands and other minds, crushing all that appears different from our own perception of right. Each person and each creature has the unequivocal right to their own mental, physical, and spiritual space here on earth as a continuity with the before and with the future.

The physical is lost first with any form of aggression, then the mind and the heart are attacked. Basic customs, concepts, and even roads to You in houses of worship are crushed or distorted. Let us share our inner strengths with those struggling for freedom, the basic ingredient of the Soul.

We must be careful not to liken negative deeds and compound them with our own in the name of "right." Let us begin to develop the ultimate power of persuasion, that which is the Inner Source in all of us. Nothing is near to it in lasting strength. We must begin to discover this Source and learn to direct it to those in need. This is our show of strength and one day in time it will be the ultimate power, that of love and acceptance, understanding and knowledge.

Peace will come only when respect is a mutual way of life for only then will we make way for the other roads to knowledge. Knowing love will answer all territorial needs, in that we will have found our own space as part of the Whole Body of Life, independent and totally free, while belonging to the total sphere.

Do we all not just want to find our own place? A place for us to be free, yet secure, to be loved and to love in return? Unfortunately, we disguise it in the debris of daily doings left unfulfilled by shallow dreams.

Reach out to seek the Light and be silent to hear the sounds of the Morning Sun. The journey to peace starts on the borders of ourselves, gradually traveling not over mountains and seas to right the wrongs, but inward to begin to know what it is all about. Peace is not on a piece of paper or the opposite of aggression. It is inside each of us. This is the only place where it can be found and nourished and ultimately shared.

Death

Time passing with great speed, where are you going? Will this brief encounter of a few short decades be our total, or will life continue as it has come? Did it arrive from another time or begin its reality on this plane?

We come to love and feel comfortable with a few around us and even though we sometimes try to possess them out of desperation, their presence in this life is most valued for mental or physical security. What of these? They are taken from us at unpredictable and questionable times. The void is a cavern carved in our hearts scarring the tissue with a crevasse of loneliness.

How are we to deal with this when we are helplessly out of control? You have said that we have choice, but here, it seems there lies none. If we could only glimpse beyond to see what awaits us. Is it darkness or will we bask in Your Light no matter how we have faltered?

Morning Glow, rising to protect us and cover us with Your warmth. Will You be there when life ends and have You been there in the "before?" You are ever present and everlasting, Time Eternal itself. You are time and not separate from it. Therefore, You are with us now and have carried us from then to beyond our mental barriers. So limited is our vision of You that we fail to recognize Your encompassing of the Whole. You are what is and what was and what will be. We travel parallel to You on different paths in time always in reach of Your Presence.

If we have indeed come from You in the before and if we travel with You now, although blind, we will, as time sees fit, come to see You again in your full Presence when our breath flees us and our functions lie still. Should we not then celebrate the passing of those we love and mourn? Should we not rise in joy from lonely pain and gives thanks that they are once again free from limited physical and mental bonds to fly home to You? Is this not why we struggle so desperately to accomplish the good?

In the "after" there is a gathering of all whom we have loved and held dear. Let us look beyond our own personal loss in the passing of a fellow traveler and rise to praise your embracing of them for You are Time Eternal and pass with them and we through the journeys.

We seem to have no control or choice as time dictates our pace. Yet, can we not come home to You sooner through recognition of Your Presence? I have begun to know You and in this time I have learned that my passing will only be a transition from a limited body to a knowing Spirit and I will be free again to travel in Light and Knowledge. During my time here I will proceed to seek the mystery that is You. But, I will never again come to look at death as an end, but only a beginning.

We should not seek death either as a means to You for only in life and through its lessons will we begin to grow closer to You. Let us learn to relax with the passing of time and those close to us. Let us learn to accept its presence as we accept Yours, everlasting and forward moving. It is alright to reach the end of the journey and we no longer should fear it. Let us try in every way to help prepare those less agile and more helpless than we; those confined by age in their bodies and minds. Let us make their way as easy as possible and return them to dignity in order to prepare them for the journey home to You.

This peaceful passing we call death is only preceded by fear. Its actual presence and time beyond are all part of the Light filled with peace and harmony and the knowledge of the Whole.

I look to the time beyond when we can be together again and while here, I will continue to seek You and to make Your Presence known.

Solstice Time

Reflections of You in the morning mist, clearing the way for daybreak. Light into day as the clouds part to herald Your glory.

In this solstice time are we to see You or only an image of Your magnificence? If You are really here at all times, why is it so often difficult to recognize Your Presence? Your glow is blinding. We can teach ourselves to look at You in order to really see. Each ray reflects You and Light itself is proof of Your Presence.

Help me to know You and see You and feel Your Presence every day of my time here. Clear the clustered details of daily living from my consciousness and allow me to think of You, openly seeking and accepting Your Light.

Help me to know what to do on this journey. Teach me to simplify as You are simplicity. Only by balancing can I see clearly the road to understanding the purpose of my venture.

Sometimes You are so very clear to me and all else is blanketed in fog. Although this is not balanced, it is what I look for ahead, a clear vision of You and each of us related to the Whole.

You come and go from me. How can I hold You near? Yes, I see. You are near to me at all times, and I need only to recognize Your Presence.

Spirit, fly me home soon to the end of this journey and carry with You those I have held dear so we may live in the Light together after our lessons learned here.

Sometimes I have wondered why we all have struggled so to go forward. I now know that the goals set were only signposts and the lessons learned were the reasons why. Each act of every day living holds merit towards our growth. The pain of each failure or glory of each success are quietly overshadowed by the lessons learned during the effort. Teach us to focus not on a reflected value, but the true merit of what we accomplish, that which affects the growth of the Soul.

I have been distracted and allowed You to go from me. Teach me to be conscious of Your Presence, not on shrines or in houses of worship, but in my heart each day for the rest of my stay.

Signposts

How am I to see the signposts along the way? Are they brightly colored for me to see or subdued in the camouflage of daily doings? They seem to be clear indications of directions to be taken in order to find the path home. They are not obvious and must be looked for, or at least observed when they come into view. Heavy distractions fostered in my ego blur my vision and their presence and meanings are oftentimes concealed.

Light into day—there are lessons all around me. Answers to all the questions in time are within my reach if I only but look for them and remain open to their signs.

I stumble and fall day after day fulfilling my pounds of ego. When a Ray of Light shines through and I glimpse at it, I realize the value of lessons learned. What we accomplish has little value when compared to what has been learned in the venture.

I want to learn each day of my time here lessons that will open my eyes to truly see, not as a momentary ray of hope, but as a constant guide to everyday living.

Daybreak into dawn—does the wind carry Your messages? Need I only but listen to hear Your words? Since I am You and You are me, are the messages carried within me always? Do I need but look inside to identify reality and its meanings? Am I, then, not the ultimate signpost? As I look inside of myself to recognize who I am, let me acknowledge the value of all I see and hear. Separate me from the self which reflects and responds to the other sights and sounds in the world. Seek only the me who is of the Enlightenment. We all came from Light and shall return to Light. Let me gather from the illumination in each of us a better understanding of the me who has been for the time before. This is who I really am, a compilation of all that I have been gathering and a few more lessons from the experience here and now.

The only value of the ''now'' time is what I add to the Whole. All other details, frustrations, accomplishments and such are of but momentary meaning. They all flee with my breath in time like the wind traveling but once upon a plain. It returns again not to build in substance for the wind has no foundation. So, too, these events I call important have no basis except to fulfill momentary goals. They flee with the wind and leave me either with a void or with lessons learned to add to the experience of living.

Help me to experience love in all that I do and say.

Curb the negative, selfish emotions I emit and allow them to recycle for the good of others, for in doing so, I benefit beyond measure. In giving I receive far more than I bargained for, not in material goods, but in the giving of the heart.

As I begin to recognize and accept love as well as give it, I embrace love as the concept of the Whole. Light unto Light—I share my gifts of love, and darkness will cease to be. Light will enter and illuminate us for time eternal and we will be free again to experience joy in the knowledge of why.

Reality

What is Real? Is it what we perceive when we look or what we hear when we listen? Is the object real that we touch because it is tangible and we feel touch when contact is made? What of our bodies and the egocentric frills which surround them? What of the indulgence in these, in the physical sensations of sight and sound and touch or the comforting choice of exterior fashion for our coverings? What of these? How should we value the pleasures and needs of the senses and our own image of ourself?

We come to this plane with each of these. Are we to ignore them or should we indulge them to the fullest? How are we to know the limits?

The key to insight is balance. Should we then work to balance the needs with the excesses? Is preoccupation with the sensual a negative influence in our growth or is it once again, a place where one will find him or herself at some point? Should it then be looked upon as a stage which will pass in time and which at some moment needs special focus in order to learn the lesson there. Should we then not judge another caught in a superficial web of exterior reflections? This could, indeed, be the place where they can learn most or a place where they will pass wasted time and energies seeking lessons not yet learned.

A key to enlightenment is not to judge the place where someone has paused on their pathway, for we have not known their ''before'' and cannot mentally encompass their pathway to date. Therefore, judging of even the most basic level is unjust and unfounded.

What is real is only that which transpires in our own sphere of reference—that which encompasses our relationship to the Whole. All that is around us is only a reflection from our own minds of what is momentary and passing. It has no longevity and, therefore, no real importance.

Morning Sun—I yearn to rise in Light, as You do, to the level where I can separate my own person, that which I call ''ego'' from what is real. Distractions and distorted superficial needs drive me towards the exclusion of my Inner Self, the part of me that is in connection with You and all others. Teach me to see clearly the limited and short-lived value of what I physically possess in order that I may develop a concentration on what is lasting, that which was me before, and now, and in the time to come. All that I have ever been is still with me but is overshadowed by my physical presence. Those of whom I have been in order to gain my lessons are no longer real in the physical sense, as I too, will no longer be in just a few brief moments in time.

Teach me, then, not to dwell on what I teach to others for it may be magnified in importance by them and further distort my vision of reality. Teach me the beauty of detachment which leaves me as I really am, a compilation of lessons learned and still in motion.

When we visit again after this time has passed, when we are again in full knowledge a part of the Whole. I now know that I will be separated from the me that others see. Teach me, then, not to lean on the attributes which make life so easy for one with a positive exterior presence. When all flows so easily for me, guide me to look beyond my acceptance here to what is of greater value. If I bask in the physical glory given me freely here, all that has transpired will leave me and dissipate with age and my passing. Let me recognize and learn all which is meaningful here in order that I may take it with me on my journey homeward, for lessons learned will be the only baggage allowed.

Perfection

You are Light—all else is darkness. You are the epitome of form, the optimum shape—perfection in Your never-ending circumference. We are flawed and have marred the planet You created in perfect balance. We have upset its harmony and balance.

If we are to reach perfection, how are we to attain it? Must we first look to recognize it in Your Presence? Yet, we have no hope of nearing You in Your likeness. Then what are we to pursue?

Perfection was the natural order of things at the beginning of life. Must we then look to what was and reflect on what has become? Is the sum difference what we must attain? But, we cannot go back in time when progress, as it is called, has brought us forward and much for the good. Must we look, then, to the negatives creating the imbalance—those which bear our names of greed, avarice, etc.? All they really encompass is unlovingness. If we truly have love for who we are, what we do, for those we encounter and their differences, then will we have not reversed the negatives compounded by and dressed in progress?

Let us take the moments necessary to reflect upon what has generated our state. Is it not a separateness of Spirit in face of physical possession with those we encounter? Should we not reverse the attachments and enjoy a loving separateness from those around us, all the while recognizing our ongoing and ultimate connection to the Whole? If we can, at least, see our connection with all other creatures, then we can indeed begin to reverse the negatives for even in the wake of direct physical or mental confrontation with another, our connections will shine through if we are willing to let them. Thus, when Light enters our pathway, our darkest traits are lightened and we begin to see.

Light into darkness, make me ever aware of Your Presence and awesome glow. Guide me to think of love and our connections to each other when it is most difficult; that is, in the state of agitation and confrontation. If I can but remember You and Your boundless love, then I can evaluate consciously my actions. Let me not respond with my darker instincts and guide Your Light to my shadowed places so that I may shine it in reflection to others.

Being Alone

Why is it so difficult this "being alone"? Why have I chosen a life in which I must learn to travel by myself? Although bound by love and caring, my ties are severed at the foundation bearing a feeling of solitude and aloneness. For the years here, my consciousness has sought companionship and friendship in family and friends, yet never any penetrates my walls. I chose one to whom I gave the keys to the internal lock, yet he chooses not to visit that space. He stands alone, secure in his being. Although he appears to struggle with life's tedious chores, he is calm inside with a quiet, solitary confidence. He forces me to stand as I am, no more and no less. He pursues not the "who" I might be and totally accepts the "me" as I am, sometimes more than I am capable of. It is hard, this journey. As I experience separateness as the state in which my mind lies, I remember that I am connected with others on the higher level. While here, I must identify who and why I am and who I am to become. How much longer is this journey?

The morning chill begins to dissipate in the warmth

of the sun rays. Clouds scatter after the rains and the lush green of the hillside reflects life abundance.

Guide me to identify more clearly my being; not the presence I fulfill for others in my daily roles, but the "who" that I am on the plane of continuity. Let me begin to identify and come to know the me who has gathered so many of the lessons before. Help me to begin to put them to work here in order that I might share them with others and, in turn, learn from their journeys.

I have come to believe that we choose our paths more knowingly than we may admit. Identification is usually only with peer group success and this is the chosen road we salvage as our own. But, in reality, have we not chosen the negative roads also? Are these not where our greatest lessons are learned? And those we choose to surround ourselves with, are they not selected as a necessary part of our curriculum?

When I evaluate my state of aloneness, I must see that the choice of lifestyle and life partners has been one that will enable me to reach the goals which I have planned as a result of this journey. Help me to accept my choices and to recognize in them the lessons I am to learn, for the journey would be for naught if it were paved and padded for pleasures. I must remember my choices. Sometimes, that is most difficult, for I know that many ways are open to me.

Guide me to constantly be strong enough to choose that which will foster my growth and to share my internal time only with those who will allow my changes to go unhindered.

Choice is mine before, now, and after this journey. Let me never again forget in moments of overcast that I have chosen this way and can direct my course from here, henceforth, homeward to You.

Sister Moon

Moon's reflection—how is it that I cannot see but your crescent edge? I know you are there, yet, I cannot see you. What can I learn from you, sliver of light? You are silent and still—watchful over us in the darkened night. Are you sister to the sun or is your stillness cold and unrelated? What is the spiritual purpose for your presence? What do I already know of you? Let me communicate with you.

Your presence, your purpose is one of continuity. The light in your image is the reflection of the physical source of life, the sun. Your image is ever-changing with the quarters. Is it that we sometimes see you whole and at other times see but a sliver or nothing at all? Are you a reflection and reminder that we cannot always be totally aware of the Light, the Whole? And that being aware of only a portion at times is also acceptable when our responsibilities, activities, and the like cover the rest from view? Is this it? Is this your purpose to remind us not to despair when we cannot spend the time we would like in seeking the Light and our part in the Whole? If we are but aware at times, then this is enough?

Day breaks with the brilliance of light and all creatures are gifted with warmth and natural vision. When the light leaves to end the day, are you there then to remind us that whether our awareness is only a crescent or a quarter or a half of what it might be at other times, that this is alright if indeed it is all we can do in the face of other pressures and clouds?

Let us not excuse our time away with frivolous deeds; yet, let us be tolerant of what demands are made upon us. There are even moments when you are completely blocked from view. When our mental spaces are filled with darkness let us not despair, for even on a moonless night, daybreak will always follow and the Light will rise to envelop us once again in love and understanding.

Sister Moon, you are truly a source for and a guide to enlightenment. Teach me to look to you and to much of what is around me to learn what reality is.

Daybreak into dawn, Your continuity, Spirit, warms my heart and calms my anxieties for the forthcoming day. Your unlimited love for each of us encourages me to look inward and to see what You love there. It is none of the superficialities we work to nurture each day, nor is it the success written of us by others. You love in me the love I hold for and share with others. Love likens to love and passes it continuously through time. You are time eternal and love itself.

Teach me not to lose myself in the burdens of daily living I place upon myself. Share with me the peace of mind to at least recognize Your Presence each day in the passing of the sun and under the nocturnal guardianship of the reflection of Sister Moon.

Guide me to stop at moments when all seems overwhelming and look upward. Let Your Presence serve as a reminder to me that I must separate reality from illusion and that balance is in order. When I look to You, help me remember and see Your Presence even on the darkest and most cloud filled days. Remind me that Your true Light does not shine from above, but from within each of us. Let me look inward to search for You, for I know that you await me there.

Rain

Rain—you release the stress of the parched earth filling the crevasses with liquid moisture for it to soak up and soften its crust. You are the beverage of life and a gift of the Universe. You are part of the earth and all in it. You come from the earth and return to it with never ending continuity. Do you not then represent reality—a total unity with all that is part of the Whole? A separate entity, yet consistently flowing, evaporating, misting and falling to flow once again. You, life's moisture and flexibility, are a perfect model for oneness.

Perimeter of Self

Teach me to leave "I, the doer" to search and find and be at peace with "I, who am." Let there be time in each of my days that I may leave the binding activity of my physical outer world for the freedom and space of my inner world. They are separate and my perspective on all around me will be borderless if I can recognize and come to utilize the division of these two states.

Physically, I am bound by my limitations, obligations, and inhibitions. The barriers can be lifted only so far. But, my mental spaces—consciously they are as limited as the physical perimeters. However, I can work to free them and allow myself to enter the free flight of my Inner Sky. Here, I can soar on the brilliance of colorless wings to journey through times past and present. Free from the bondage of limitations, I seek to live in the mind and beyond; to journey with Light and to exist in the knowledge of "why."

Is it possible to seek and achieve this space while captured in the necessary needs, pursuits and drives of a physical body? I want to border on the outer limits of the perimeter of this self.

Teach me to seek and to recognize who I am and to reach not for tomorrow's illusive goals, but for my part and identity in this natural order of things.

We all travel a similar road, yet the false illusion blinds each of us in varying degrees. Teach us a tolerance of others and their place on the journey for each is individual and not able to be truly seen from where we view.

Simplicity

Daylight enters the darkness of our minds—fear turns to love and hatred to tolerance and understanding. The distant Light of Knowledge breaks the horizon and the warmth of morning dissipates the frost.

Kindle the Light of love in each of us from a flicker to a flame broadening our glow and encompassing those around us.

Light, rise from the eastern sky and bring the knowledge of the ages to allow us to learn from what has already been while contemplating the ''now.''

Chant of Morning Awareness—insect pitch and treetop harmonics, You offer the gentle wind your secrets of simplicity. Carry them for all to hear in our listening moments.

I wait for the words of what has been known, growing calmer with each phrase. Learning seems so slow, so tedious, and enlightenment a million years away when life is cluttered with conformity and impersonal contributions, those not of the self.

Awareness comes only on simple paths. Break in the morning sky, burn the mist from my mind and clear my vision to select simplicity. Tune my hearing to the fine sounds of morning music, letting me hear only what is needed and dispelling illusive distractions and shallow compliments.

Simplicity in mind and Spirit is a necessary signpost on my pathway homeward. It eases and uncomplicates choices between falsehood and reality. As I simplify my life, the choices to the higher level are clearer and in less danger of confusion. As I rise to the moments when clarification is possible, I clear my mind of the debris of shallow or hurtful gestures. As I fill it with love and acceptance, I join with all other creatures to celebrate the awareness of our unity.

I am to be of the heart and of the mind and undo the locks of fear encompassing my love. I am not to be afraid for a moment's investment is neither chance nor short-lived. It is, instead, the true way of all life and continues in its rewards. Invest in myself as a loving and caring being. Awareness and knowledge will come as I realize that love is the natural order of all things as it flows from one to another, to creatures large and small, and from the Light to its reflections—each of us.

I am not to be afraid to live with love and kindness for these are what is natural to me. I have only forgotten for a moment.

Judgment

It is of little importance who sees You first, it is only important that we all grow to gradually experience Your glow. Time is of little value when we look at the overall length of the Plan. How much time is a moment in the span it takes us to be able to love and accept and learn freely? Are there not some lives that touch not a reflective thought upon any of these? And what of time passing? Does it not place life again before us as possible ways of becoming enlightened? How long we must work to gain passage Homeward. It is not the days passing that brings us closer to You, but the energies and efforts put forth during these times that will pave our paths more surely to You.

Help to enlighten my darkened mind and fill it with Light to spread and share with others. Show me the way on the road to love and kindness and when I wander, gently guide my vision back to the proper perspective of the Overall Plan. My time is spent amidst the challenges of daily living. Guide me to balance these deeds for daily survival along with the necessary lessons for learning.

Forgive me when love and kindness become only mental pillows and I fail to extend them to those I encounter in my mind or in my presence. It is so easy to judge. It is the simplest of all expressions and one which localizes peer support. The greatest of accomplishments is to learn to judge not. The road to love and kindness and ultimately knowledge, is paved not with performed facts, but with objective appraisals of our own inability to know all sides of any issue or person.

Let us seek to accept, not confront, anothers' opinion or deed. There is but folly in our judgment of the value of what others offer for we have no way of knowing where they are on their journey and what lessons they are still to learn. Of most importance, we should direct our presence towards our positive approach to life and not delete our supply of loving kindness through judgment, for judgment not only drains these from our Inner Self, but also blocks the free path to knowledge. Only openness and objectivity will part the clouds and allow the Light to warm us with its glow.

Morning Light, guide me to give myself not just in my mind filled with love, but in my every day deeds. Let me weave kindness and hope and love into my moments in time clearing my vision to better see You and to live in the knowledge of Your love.

Love and kindness are first nurtured in the mind and then often spread to the heart and shared in our deeds. Let me blend with my life what I have learned and hoard it not for personal solitude for only in sharing knowledge will it be open for additional expansion.

Detachment

Thank you for the Rays of Golden Light, the Rays of Knowledge You shed with each passing day. It is as if we have all been asleep and are now awakening slowly and cautiously to music of morning melodies.

The connections are being made and recognized on this brink of enlightenment. Have I ever been so filled with hope? As the fragments begin to blend together, it is obvious that they are threads of love and lessons and learning that bring us together.

Let us lend love to those around us who are under the glow of the growing intensity. When they are unsure, let us give assurance; when they falter, let us give stability; when they fear, let us give unmeasured love to cushion the pain.

We ourselves must learn that detachment from others is the first step towards total love and acceptance of them. We must detach not our love but our need to take from or reflect on them. Leave us free to respond to who they really are and not who we imagine them to be, for only in total acceptance can we truly love what is rather than a draining reflection of our needs.

I have found that life's lessons are indeed in those around me. Total love and understanding is the connection of mind and spirit with my mother; the symbols of learning and guidance are indeed the basic thirst and fiber of my sister; tolerance and acceptance is the reflection of my brother; and the challenge and wonder of growth from he whom I chose as a fellow traveler.

Even without the conscious knowledge, he teaches me detachment and objectivity. He brings the most difficult of lessons, but also paves the way for my totally free commitment to all others. My days are blessed with what each of them surrounds me with.

Teach me to be aware of the lessons and to recognize the bearers of these truths as fellow travelers on the journey.

Teach me to dispel the roles we fabricate for each other on this plane and allow me to begin to see them as they really are. For them I am eternally grateful not just for their presence and challenges, but for the recognition of such.

We are on the brink of the dawn of a new age of enlightenment. Let us enter into it together and turn to shed as much of the rays of hope and love to others as we can.

Free us of the mental bonds of our surrounding values and let us be peaceful in our pursuit of You. The Light is with us always. We must only be awake to be aware of its Presence in us and in all others. This is the Unity. After initial detachment comes the truly complete connection bound by love and learning, acceptance and change. For these four gifts in person I am truly grateful for You have surrounded me with obvious signposts. Let me progress the farthest possible on my journey during this time encompassed by love.

Responses

Pain and sorrow, fear and despair—innkeepers of our minds and bodies. Must we travel the journey with these constantly battling the Presence? Can life be not joyful and exciting? Can we not approach a day without these negative influences?

We do all we can to negate Your Presence and avoid Your recognition. What approach should we take? How should we see this?

The roads are paved with signposts. Are You but one of them? If we are not to avoid You, should we then try to recognize Your purpose in the overall scheme? How are we to differentiate what is for learning and what is self-imposed for pity and escape?

The confusion is sometimes overwhelming. Where do we decipher the line between a lesson to be learned and self-indulgence? Is there no such line? Can there possibly be lessons learned in both? Are we too harsh on ourselves and others in judgment of the handling of these? How are we to respond to pain and sorrow, fear and despair? And what of our response to others? Should we just accept or inter-cept their process? Is accepting not just proliferating and is interfering not just a response to our biased judgment of the situation? What are we to do for ourselves and others? I await the answer and it comes.

Take hold of your judgment and judge not. The road to what is true is paved with honesty. Search your own mind for the honest evaluation of your actions, deeds, and indulgences, for only you can fully see what is real and what is true. You may decide to banish these truths, but only you have the choice to do so. If this is not your time to recognize what is real, then it will come in another moment. As for others, we can only guide them to honesty as we can see it. They then must make their determination if the pain is real, or worthwhile, or in need of banishment from their lives. The same for sorrow, fear and despair. Judge not others in their pursuits and indulgences for what might appear to be the latter could indeed be a conquest long overdue.

Extend love and hope, kindness and acceptance to each other and these will come in time to negate the rest for knowledge through example will proliferate and all will come to see. Let us be patient with one another in the interim.

A New Day

A new day is coming when all will be clear. The Light will flow unobstructed into the dark spaces of our minds and hearts and we will all be aglow with it's knowledge and brilliance. Soon, the clouds of night will clear for the dawn of the new day when all have vision. They will be able to see what is real and what is of value.

Love and peace will fill us all and we will live in harmony. All will know balance, and the illusion of good and evil in life will appear openly on the scales for all to observe. Judgment will be made not, but a clear evaluation of deeds accomplished will benefit our continued growth.

Is this the morning of the last day of this life of which we speak? Or can it possibly be a day, any day, which I choose during this journey? Can we truly live with an acknowledgment of the Light in us, sharing it with others? Can we really help others know once we have opened our own minds? Is it possible to evaluate reality from illusion on this plane? Can we surround our space with harmony just by living in non-judgment of others? Can this peace be achieved so easily when we dispel conflicts of will and judgment? Can I now look beyond me to whom I might be and work not to create a new person, but to unlock the original one now trapped in my ego.

This state of harmony can be achieved on this plane with the willful mindfulness of our actions evolved in love and kindness and hope for others.

Remind me each morning with the rising sun that I possess the ability to accomplish this state. I need only desire to and it will be mine.

The beauty in the delight of the child discovering a flower for the first time is in the total acceptance of its magnificent presence in sight, touch and smell, free from performed expectations. The response is natural, free from bonds of controlled, anticipated response. The incredible innocence of acceptance and total trust . . . where was it lost along the way so very young on the path of this life? Perhaps some cannot even remember and others will never see. Yet, there are those who can and will return to their place in the natural order of things.

Spirit, carry me on the wings of change so that I will learn again detachment from all that will pass in a short while. Free me from the bondage and pain of attachment so that I may ''just be'' as I really am and grow from the insights I have gathered. Widen my vision from the narrow tunnel I safely call my life and open it to encompass what is really lasting. Relieve me of the burden of forcing life to occur in a specific way for this is my illusion of control and totally dominates my freedom.

Crystal Light of Love, teach me freedom from attachment in order that I may no longer live in expectations. Free me, in turn, to give love and acceptance and to be mindful of all that is not real.

Attitudes

Is it not the hour to confront the attitudes that envelop us? Time passes and moments are wasted deciphering and responding to emotional patterns we have plotted for our self-made designs. We have woven into the fibers guilt and fear, desire and dependence. We have learned to clutch and grab for a connection in life. This image of ego we call identification, is it not but a composite of self-fulfilling neurosis? Have we not set the stage filled with molded roles that we now need only play out to be fulfilled? And at the end of our brief performances, have we indeed found fulfillment in free expression of self or have we merely played a prefabricated role to the satisfaction of others and our ego-based self?

How deep does the individuality in each of us lie? How much debris and how many prefabricated barriers must be removed before we can discover "Self" in the freedom of our living Spirit? The roles, the needs, the desires, the fears and expectations; do they all not expect the results, reality, to happen in a specific way, or will disappointment and unrest not encompass us in a negative aura? Can we not separate ourselves from these binding mental barriers we ourselves have set before us? One must know freedom to desire it, and with this accomplished, is it possible to reach a state of detachment in order to respond to life in a natural, free flowing manner, separate from unexpected responses, accomplishments, and results?

Think for just a moment of the possibilities of being free from motivations into which we have submerged our true identity. What a joy to respond to nature and our fellow creatures for the first time without preconceived motives or anticipated results. Could not the uninhibited joy of a child blissful at play be ours once again? And what of those few rare moments that we have truly felt love? Could we not enjoy them on a continuing basis by just giving love instead of only receiving it as before? Does this extension of ourselves not bring satisfaction on the highest level? And what of contentment? Is this not a most contagious state as is anxiety and neurosis? Then why not extend the influence we have on each other beyond the negatives into the area of Light encompassing love, acceptance, kindness, and even sometimes, understanding?

Love only bears love as does its likeness in kindness and the rest. It can never breed a negative by virtue of itself alone. Other responses may be ridden by uneasy and questionable fears or guilts; but, this is limited by virtue of itself for it is only a response to what we think is real and not reality itself.

We cannot expect all to either understand or to follow and this is where our final understanding must dominate. But, for those of us who can at this time recognize the possibilities of change and excite in the exploration of who we really are minus the self-styled trimmings, there is much with which to rejoice. The challenge is overwhelming; yet, the goal is attainable for time has no measure, only in our mental entrapment. When we can free ourselves of the barriers of beginning and end, goal and accomplishment, reaction, action and reaction again, then the concept of life and death will also fade from our self-styled imaginings.

Time passing is the flow of life in unity with the Whole who is time eternal itself. When the doors of our mental spaces are unlocked and we are once again free to travel in thought and deed, unhampered by ''survival,'' then we will once again know peace for in the total vulnerability of ''being'' we will come to recognize our true identity as a totally free Spirit in the glow of the Light.

Come, let us fly together in the Morning Light of the Dawn of Enlightenment.

The Connection

Good Morning, Good Morning. When all else seems disconnected, my unity with You beyond this plane seems strongest. Why do we only look in desperate hours for the bonds which are naturally ours?

Magnificent Light, You kindle in each of us the glow of hope and kindness and love. Why do we only see this in moments of separateness from our daily lives? Are they so very cluttered that all of our energy must be spent muddling through?

When I am quiet, there is a great sense of Your Presence around me—guiding, protecting, and loving. If I could only retain this awareness throughout my days of this journey.

Teach me to remember that loving-kindness is the bond we share. We all want to love and be kind and giving by our very nature. The barriers to these gifts are oftentimes insurmountable for many of us and we never quite touch the reality of our own nature. We remain "victimized" by our surroundings and environment.

Remind me in times of confusion and distraction, that separating from meaningless values will make me ever mindful of our unity. Guide me to see my true connection with others, as part of the Universal One.

I can help myself and others to see the bond and rejoice in the connection by living with love and kindness and understanding for all, regardless of personal conflict. If I cannot understand, then at least let me bear tolerance and respect for the differences. In friendship lies the possibilities of all three. An openness of heart and mind will foster the basic connection and lead me to unity.

In enlightened moments I find the ultimate in friendship (ever loving, kind by nature, understanding and accepting) all to limits beyond my comprehension. Let me look to the higher aspects of myself for the passage of these gifts of the Spirit through me to others, in turn, sharing the Light.

Spirit, teach me to be ever aware of what I have to offer to others and less mindful of what I will receive for love and friendship is giving, not a trade.

Attachments

I won't apologize for days past, lost in distraction; nor will I delude myself or You with future promises. I am just at peace to be here now, experiencing the morning and rebirth of the new day, a new beginning of life.

This new day and this new age of consciousness bring with them new challenges as well as joys to the spirit. Let me test the waters of Your stream a little more each day, stumbling at times on the irregular, unforeseen rocks, while all the time renewing my thirst for the timeless answers.

What a joy to know but a few moments when the mind is at rest and releases its registration of the debris there. I yearn for clarity, simplicity, and a mindfulness of the moments which make up change. Change, constant change, is the way of time. How have we come to fight it so?

The ego in each of us claims rule and, therefore, deluges our mind with attachments to unresolved persons and problems, both past and future, oftentimes overwhelming the present. We, therefore, easily lose sight of the changes which encompass all things. We clutch and grab hold of that which is recognizable to us, regardless of the pain and suffering it brings.

Attachment to times past and possibilities in the future are illusive and have no tangible satisfaction related to growth. Growth can only be accomplished journeying through change. It can be a soothing flow of the river carrying us on the journey if we only untie the lines that attach us to the shoreline of stagnation.

How is it that we do not remember that the journey will be swifter, more joyful, and certainly more spontaneously exciting as we free ourselves from the past and let the future be?

The ego in each of us that questions our immortality and continuity clutches to those events and persons tangible in our current life to gain a stable base and reason for being here. As a result, we are often overwhelmed with attachments.

Let us learn the way to free ourselves of the pain we ourselves hold onto. The journey on the river homeward will only begin when we consciously decide to let go of what has been or might be and begin to celebrate the now of each moment of each day.

The river is swift and smooth flowing and it knows

the way Home. Let us open our minds and allow its currents to cleanse us of attachments as we experience a free flow of faith.

The Seasons

The seasons flow as the river and time eternal itself.

Summer is the warm security of life's abundance, secure in its lush pastures as the home is to the child. All experiences new and exciting—life seems everlasting until we are told otherwise and channeled into the tunnel of a role.

Fall arrives in the middle years when the roles have been chosen and unchartered ends have been tied or clipped to secure our patterns of stereotypes we have accepted or oftentimes mold. We have accomplished something. We are not sure what, but agree that it doesn't matter, as long as we have accomplished roles of sorts.

Winter finds us looking back at how summer and fall could have been better spent when time and possibilities seemed endless. Often we hold on even tighter to the seasons past as if to insure against the inevitability of the future. The season ends on this brief journey—all seems permanent and sometimes regrettable, sometimes not.

Spring is the moment in time passing that holds new birth in life beyond this plane. Have we forgotten in lives past that there will always be rebirth, a new day, a new sunrise to fill us with new possibilities and new ways to progress on the journey homeward?

The seasons cannot be regulated or stopped, even for a moment in time. Are we the seasons? Our change is constant and flowing. How sad it is that we do not recognize ourselves as part of time and change for it will all come to pass even without our recognition.

When we come to embrace change, only then will we begin to enjoy the journey Homeward for it flows as the river, constantly in motion and passing just once each moment in time.

Nature and all things natural hold the answers. In the seasons are the patterns of life's flow. We are the seasons and they portray nature and time eternal itself. Let us look to the seasons and rejoice in their possibilities.

The Mandala

The long journey homeward is filled with distractions of mind and body which easily divert our paths. I want my journey to be clear and my vision unmarred as I search for peace, yet the distractions are repetitious. How do I filter my thoughts, guide my actions, and monitor my deeds to keep sight of my goal? Should my journey be one of isolation, or must I interact to complete the circle of love and understanding? All things we learn are stepping stones to line the path and the seasons are reflections of us and the changes we encounter.

Teach me the flow of life in order that I might accept what the days bring all the while letting go of what has passed in my mind and body. Youth leaves with no permission and the joy of aging is in the acceptance of new found knowledge, not privileged, for the young. Letting go of the desire for youth will free us to discover the joys of time passing. All is change. We are change and change is us. Only when we can come to accept and even greet it will we begin to feel peaceful.

Let me learn to let go and forgive what was yesterday borne in memories. What happened was of value at the moment in time it occurred; then, it was processed, changed and was gone. All that remains is my memory of it and any residue of pain or healing alone bear the burden of carrying it through time. It can be gone in a moment if I truly desire it to be so, for I create reality within my own sphere and I only allow others to affect it as much as I permit.

I can come to the constant, not momentary, realization that all that happens can and will affect me only to the extent that I allow. I, therefore, have the complete ability to discard that which is excess baggage in my mind and crowds the mental spaces there. I can, also, avoid living in expectations of what will come in the future, thereby avoiding disappointment when my false expectations of reality are not met to my liking or timing.

What then is left to fill me? Help me be free and open to what is happening now, the only moment of reality that counts. Let me not run past the flowers, or judge those seemingly failures I encounter. Let me think only of the beauty in each living creature and recognize their place of importance in the overall plan. None are less or more important than the others. When confrontation in thought or deed surround my ego, let me search for understanding even if knowledge of their "why" cannot be found, then let me lay the way for acceptance and trust in the fact that their path is not mine and I can never see completely the map of their journey while here.

Let me work within the mandala of love and kindness, knowledge and acceptance. Let me do all that I can to allow others to enter also if it is where they can be for this life is a cycle in the flow of everlasting change. Let me tap into the mandala and make my way in truth while I search for the Light. Let me make my way around the mandala as I search for the place of endings and beginnings.

Kindness

Thank you for the Morning Light, the glow of a new day for each of us, the plants, the creatures and we who co-exist with them as part of the Whole. Let us each absorb the Light and life You so generously abound us with. You are the Source of all existence and strength. Force which does not emanate from You is filled with falsehood and illusion.

Teach us to be kind enough and to love ourselves enough to accept Your gifts. Why are we so hard on ourselves? Why do we allow our vulnerability to prejudice, disease, and other negative realities to be so constant? Can we not but spare a moment of joyful loving-kindness for the one whom we are? Why have we evolved to believe that this is not the way to peace? We are taught only outward directions, when indeed, the Source of all love and understanding lies in You within us. Truly, it is manifested in others, but first must be recognized and nurtured in each of us.

Why have we made this living so difficult for ourselves by placing ourselves last in line for consideration of love? We have come to believe that the love for us will come from another, one outside of ourselves who also wanders about in search of the bearer of his or her love.

How have we patterned ourselves so far off course that we do not recognize Your Source of all love lies within us? We are part of the composite of Your Whole. Love can only generate from within and go outward for us to truly feel its warmth and joy. Love borne from others and given to us is our connection with them as part of Your Whole, but it is not and will never be our Source of life and love.

Teach us that we must first come to appreciate the we who we are part of and only then can we begin to share our love with others.

We search our whole time here for responses from parents, lovers, children and pets when these and other friends should be but a reflection of our giving from their own Source of Light. Disappointment will abound if we look to them to respond in a way we deem fulfilling to make us feel loved, for Your love is not an item or a gift, but a state of being. Your love liquefies and passes away prejudice and disease, desires and disappointments. Let us but love ourselves a little more than we have and allow ourselves the tolerance we do generously expect others to share.

Joy, joy at a new day of living. It would be much easier for all to bear if we only allowed ourselves to respond to what we are naturally in an unprocessed way. Let us learn from the abundant beauty of the flowers and the simple existence's of the smaller creatures. They live with nature and allow no false expectations of imagery. They exist totally from Your abundance, totally accepting of the natural way.

Spirit, why have we strived so to separate ourselves from this way which is also ours? Is it that we seek higher enlightenment? I think not. We but seek recognition and possession of a place in this time, both stemming from outside of ourselves. Our pursuits are shallow and ultimately filled with illusion if these alone are our endeavors.

Let us look again to the natural way, seeking Your peace as our only goal and all other pursuits as our intention. Letting go of our attachments to the outcome of our efforts allows us to experience peace of mind, and the Inner Peace in all of our endeavors.

Teach us the simplicity of the flower that grows to its fullest magnificence with only Your Light and moist earth. It is solely preoccupied with growing to the fullest beauty that it might be. And, if then, others can share its experience, this is joyful giving, but indeed not a priority. Let us look to nature and its many lessons for the answers are all around us.

Teach me to keep my vision and goals clear as the flowers do and I will be assured that my petals will unfold in Your magnificent Light. When I am achieving my fullest, others can also feel my abundance. Let this always remain in the order of importance You have planned for me as I so easily become distracted along the way.

Let me learn to love myself enough and to tend to my inner needs all the while accepting Your bountiful love. Let me learn again to be kind to myself.

The Gathering

Let us gather together in this space and time to share the common bond of knowledge that binds us as one. From the far corners of this planet minds are gathering the knowledge of who we are and why we are. Time eternal and nature hold the secrets of life and the answers are all around us.

There are now many more than before who are able to begin to see the Light. They envision through various cosmetic and cultural differences the same concept of the Universal One. We make time ourselves bordering it with incidents to give it relativity. We, too, can stop its influence. Even though the flow continues, its value is of our own selection.

Let us travel our journeys alone, yet together, in this time of Light when darkness is more omnipresent than ever. Is it not interesting that both forces are stronger than ever in this time? We each choose the way of our own commitment. The darker forces of envy and greed, power and consumption can take hold in the subtlest of ways. Negative forces need not be found in aggressive, selfish acts alone or in those highlighted by differences in culture and philosophical thought. The basic principles upon which we base our daily lives and fulfill our activities and goals indicate the direction we have taken.

Let us learn to evaluate the motives behind our deeds and to be honest about their sources.

Let us never forget that we have the ability to change that which we see and that which is relative to us.

Let us not fall victim to the concept that we are a result and not an overt action. We have choice and our perception of change is individualized, not patterning any other creature.

Let us be free enough to be creative enough to design our own road to You, for we do anyway on another plane.

Let us be conscious of our freedom of mental choice which can never be taken from us, only given away. If our bodies and space are bound in chains and woven by deceptions, we can even then be totally free for our minds are at our disposal to fly us to freedom or keep us in bondage.

Freedom of choice and change is, like love, a state of being. Each carries it through the journey and has the right to tap into or discard it at any moment. Teach us to recognize our freedom of thought and choice and let us never forget again that it is ours alone, completely now and for eternity.

Oneness

I am grateful to be awakened again in this time and space. The glories of unification in oneness are why we are here; to discover that connection and go forth with its message and implications. The journey or life, follows the road to awareness, each step we take for a higher end than we now know.

Free the Spirit in each of us to transfer those energies tediously spent into the fruitful pursuits of our higher goals. Time is the boundary we ourselves set. There is no escape from its pressures lest we sever our sense of reality concerning it. Diffuse its importance and dissipate its threats in a changing perception. I alone can challenge and master its holds on my existence. To be free from these self-imposed boundaries is to be able to consciously involve myself in the emergence of the self, ever flowing, change into change.

When the pressures of each day weigh as pounds upon our minds, let us think of time as our freedom, not captor. Let the knowledge of the continuity of life pass us over the daily stress all the while recollecting the whole perspective, ever growing and always changing for the higher enlightenment of all beings.

Let us share the peace we feel in moments of awareness with those we encounter. And, even though their knowledge may be blocked, let us seek to share the feeling of those moments filled with peace and void of words. They will share in the moment unbeknownst as to where or what it is. Just the aura of non-violence and alignment will be enough to settle each at rest in a fragment of time filled with peace. When they share it again at another time, they will come to recognize it as familiar, and will gradually discover their innate ability to generate it themselves, thereby causing others to pause in the Light.

We must learn to pass the Light from one to the other. It is rejuvenated as it touches another and the glow is heightened. If it is kept to oneself, it will be isolated and lay dormant in self-indulgence.

Share the Light of love and the knowledge of connection. It is all that is sane and real.

The Dream

Light shines on the water as a constant reminder that You are ever present. Even the moonglow reflects Your reality.

Remind me during the times when I feel that I am alone, that I need but to glance at You and remember Your magnificent Light.

Amidst the fever of a dream I saw the magnificent Source of Your Energy. All cares and emotions, save love, were taken from my shoulders at the moment of transition from this life to the next. On the journey, awareness was real and complete. Joy and knowledge blended in a weightless knowingness that freed me of doubt and from wandering.

Of those around me on the journey, some were knowing and the others fearful. You showed me that I am to embrace those who are afraid by passing onto them the confidence of transition. How will I do this?

Love and trust will abound and belief will come easily to those who are ready for the knowledge. For those who are not, the message will be but one of the many they will store but not react to until their time of enlightenment has come.

I am not to fear for who will or will not hear, for it has no relevance. I am to share my knowledge of the Light and the journey. It is mine to share. I will therefore, go into the world to give love and to share the messages as they come. There are many to help me. I will not be afraid for Your Light lives within me as in all creatures of the earth.

Spirit, help me carry the message and release it from my clutching heart to share with others for alone it will go unfulfilled. Teach me to give without fear of rejection or attachment. Teach me what real giving is and let me never look back to count those I may have touched—only forward home to You.

The Message of Love

L ove must be shared lest it be lost in distractions and self-preoccupation. The journey is long and hard and oftentimes confusing. Save love, there is little that is lasting to soften the trip. Love that comes from deep in the heart first found its place in the Soul—the Spirit traveling through time.

The message of love is one that unfolds over time —slowly releasing its rays of hope and light and knowledge to our conscious minds. It is that which is the Source of all life. Some lives are lived in darkness never knowing even a ray of Light; yet in time, all will come to know its warmth and brilliance. For those in darkness the journey is confusing and in total distraction, bound by attachments and unfulfilled goals.

The Light shines and lives in all. May I never forget that the darkest of creatures is also of the Light and if I look past the negative barricades of time that I will be able to see their Light and the reflection in my eyes and heart will be theirs to view perhaps for the very first time.

Love breeds love and is born and nurtured from

tolerance and acceptance. Let me lay down the anxieties and frustrations in this life to seek and foster love all the while remaining unattached to the act and its results.

I am bordering on the edge of time for I now have a dual consciousness. This can no longer be laid aside as "an interesting possibility." It is now my journey to live in love.

The journey is long and often narrowed by the borders of my mind. I will live to broaden my scope to encompass and envision the Light living inside of me.

Spirit, friend of my flight, help me to journey homeward in view of Your message, "Love binds all wounds, softens all roads, and frees the soul to fly home in peace."

Love's Journey

I don't know what to do with Love, but to give it away. It flows as a fountain from my heart, freely —unobstructed by pain or worry of return.

It flows outward, swiftly carrying the experience of my days and journeys from past to present. To live in love is the final stage of growth here on this plane. It once again joins the naturalness of peaceful surroundings with the conscious mind—a blending to welcome the Spirit home again into the body of the journeyer.

Love finds its way through the twisted days of our lives submerging and emerging as the tides ebb in our life.

A journey of love is one filled with a peace dwelling quietly amongst the confusion. Life's journey is what we make of it; whether it be a stormy trip or one filled with flowers and lighted pathways, we choose the plateau. We can, too, choose to change that level at any time. Yet, when one finally walks in peace, there is little else to choose as this burden called life is most easily journeyed from the soul.

To touch the heart of another traveler and to lighten their load but a limited bit brings the greatest of joy to me and pleasures untold. I yearn but for a moment and an opportunity in time to be there to reach out and touch another's soul and to somehow generate a ray of Light and a glimmer of hope in the possibilities of love.

Clear my way to journey only in Light always keeping close to my heart love that is ready to share. Light, come dwell in me so that as I commune with others, you will be there for them to see to light their way Home to You.

Love breeds love and proliferates itself from soul to soul. It is what connects us all. The Universe is One and its fiber is woven from love.

PART TWO

The Search for Self

The Cocoon

It is a quiet, dark time now when I must interpret and put into daily practice that which I have learned to be true. There is no lifelong fulfillment in my deeds, no pinnacle where I thought I would be; sharing with others what I have learned. Agony overcomes me at times with the frustration of not moving forward. What am I to do in this time of turmoil?

It is now that I must remember that the small and seemingly insignificant deeds of each day appear to have little value; yet, they are like layer upon layer of the feathers that make up magnificent wings—each has value and each an important place in making up the whole.

Life was never promised in any particular form; I have just expected it to be so. Each action has merit if it is in the direction I desire. Each, as the feather, does not have glamour or excitement attached to it; but, together, they will make up the ''me'' that is radiant and growing.

Don't be fooled by the illusions covering other lives. They are designed to project this outward, even when it may not be so. By the very nature of their design, they are illusive and shallow. But, for those living these dreams, it is their time to do so.

For me, it is not. I am at the moment in my time when I am shedding my illusive layers, a cocoon of sorts, and from it emerging as the butterfly.

The daily acts of learning to live and love and share and accept will be my food for enlightenment. I will feign distractions and be tolerant of myself as I have chosen this way and will not fight what I know in my heart to be right.

Gifts of the Light

The words have come to me as gifts of the Light. They are now to be shone, not quieted. I will pass these words on to others as a vehicle of love for all.

Nature is the map for the answers to the treasures of time. Converge upon he who knows the Light from within himself and shines it outward; the one who knows the children. He who is comfortable with the Source will show me the way to release my offerings, now that I recognize them as mine.

I won't be afraid for love is with him all the while. He will release my levers of love and the bounty will flow. As I love the Source with all of my heart, I too will be able to love all others, creatures large and small. I am capable and ready; it is but left to do. I go in peace as he awaits me. I go to him who has loved me for all time.

Windsong

Valley of light beyond the shadow of the moon—
light force enters and radiates the natural way.
Feathered white doves radiate the sun's eminence.
Nature abounds. The balance is near perfect before
we begin our motorized day. Wind songs gently
nudge all awake. The flowers turn and unfold to greet
us. The animals and their young raise their heads, so
knowing of Your valued Presence.

Teach us to look to the natural way to capture once
again life as it was created and to ultimately free us
from our synthetic world.

Passages in Time

Clear my mind, Morning Sun, as You clear the morning mist. Make my way one of total clarity and when confusion and distraction mar my path, help me to differentiate reality from illusion.

Time tested are the ways of humankind, yet this brief period is but a drop in the ocean of eternity. Many have come and many will come again who have known the Light, yet the patterns of living are still in darkness.

Pass this way another time, Gift of Light, and guide us to open our eyes and hearts to Your Glow.

Conquests

Trust in the love of the Source which will intervene the dark forces which envelop the earth planes. It will calm the seas and the air and clear the lanes of destructive energies. There are many who seek conquest. They will conquer illusions for real power lies not with territory and influence, but deep in the heart of every being. Here lies the strength of all who recognize its Source. None can be dominated if led from within the heart.

Seekers

Time passes, holding us to it. Love beckons all to fly freely. Journeyers into the night, we travel in time only in our minds besetting our futures with barriers to the truth. To live in time is to hold solid a cloud vapor. Truth is not bordered by descriptions, but boundless and ever changing according to our level of perception.

Love, join us together as seekers of truth and make our flight a journey always directed toward You, yet free to encompass all who seek with us. And of those who do not yet know what they seek, shed Your Light from us to them at the darkest of times.

Let me journey with one who knows the way. Let our minds blend together as our hearts tune as one—always unattached, yet connected in Oneness. Let the love flow unconditionally towards each other and outward to all others.

Guide us to seek only You and in doing so, find comfort and love in all whom You have created.

Love binds us as the wind binds the air, as the sea binds the shore, as the sky touches the earth. Let us follow Your Light always in view of Your Rays. Let us never forget Your direction for us, and when we falter, gift us with Your strength to help us strengthen one another.

We have chosen to journey together. How great a gift that You have offered us the road together. Let us never forget this gift of friendship that binds us, as old as time and forward moving, always growing for a greater understanding of You.

Children of Light

Motion—love in motion—light in motion—change, constant change. Millions of parts interacting as the whole—blending, intertwining. Fragmented thoughts and lives trying to differentiate reality from the illusive mists of life. Attempting to make sense of who we are, what we are, and why we are.

Two have touched in time. Children of Light, we are still not sure of the rules, but will come to realize that there are really none. The words and directions are written only in our hearts, now filled with confusion. But soon we will come to know the meanings we see there and the signposts will be illuminated for us to see.

We are afraid, but must fear not for love is with us all the while. We are love and love is us. We are separate, yet one, and the love of the Source binds us forever.

The Teacher

Making our way through these valleys and mountains of life is one of constant searching for the Source, which is ever present—all around us in what we touch and see, what we hear and envision.

Time tested are our pursuits in other directions which have proven shallow and illusive. Waive the mist of ego from our vision and free us to pursue a journey filled with Light.

It is very difficult in times like these to be totally trusting of Your directions for us. We both fight and attempt to twist Your words away from the more pleasurable path, when indeed that is the road You wish us to take for in these simple joys we can share together, there is much to expand our awareness of self, each other, all others and You.

Teach us to not be so unloving to ourselves and be our teacher of the flow of life, the river of love that continues eternally in joy and giving. Never again let us doubt Your wishes for You are our guidance through the mist into the Light of the eternal day.

Wind Dancer

Power rises in the force of daybreak, beams of light break the dawn. Wind dancer, the folklore of time, recorder of life; the only witness to our full evolution.

The wind knows no limitations and has no boundaries. It thrashes and tears, whips and whirls, daring to plot the course of natural movement. It is free, it is motion, it is Spirit in form.

We seek the heights above our plane, earthbound no more. Humans seek the stars, an inner frustration to fly as a free spirit falsely fulfilled in a mechanical mode.

I will seek not the stars and universal expeditions, but travel the ultimate journey without vehicles. The final power will transport me on the internal journey homeward.

Metamorphosis

Stop to smell the flowers for in each petal is a lesson to unfold. The answers are all there in its metamorphosis from seed of love to joyful fulfillment of unconditional giving. It asks nothing in return, just to "be."

Variations beyond comprehension and man's impression of the reality of color, assisted only by the rainbow. Nature's duo in chromatic expression.

Stop to smell the flowers, to touch and to see and to share their wealth. They are the treasures at the end of the rainbow and are fully connected with the fibers of love.

Pass their gifts from one to another and peace and harmony will once again flow on earth.

The Islands

Reflections on the water mirror images of the light while the sun energizes your being.

The sands warmth caresses your skin and blankets it with comfort while the sea cools and carries you.

The warm evening breezes bear messages from nature's knowing heart to fill your mind with new enlightenment.

Open skies and deep horizons promise space for your spirit to soar when it can let your body lie.

From the woman you hold I wish you the most fulfilling gifts she can offer. May she touch your heart and you hers while you search and journey into each other.

And from the flowers that embrace and lace the Islands, I give you a moment of love with every petal you stop to touch or see—for I am them and they are me.

Thoughts on Love

If I love you above all others, it is because you have awakened in me capabilities for that much more love.

If I am to love all whom God has created as equal, then let me not love you less to lower you to their level, but let me love them more and use you as a guiding light for my potential.

As I love God, I will seek to love you, and as my capacity to love grows, so will my awareness of love in others.

You are a luminescent catalyst for my love and for you I will be forever grateful.

Flying

Spirit, I want to journey with You into Light never again to know darkness or the weight of the human form. Fly with me, to where forms and minds are free. The air carries me as I direct my journey, bound no more by distance or material weight. Let me return to what I really am, a spirit form and part of all that is.

The sun's rays touch me and I am connected with You, separate no more. My way is filled with desires to be free from this form and from the solid state in which we live.

Teach me to accept and recognize who I am now and what I am to accomplish through Your design in order that I may return to You with great speed.

I accept—for that is what is, and I release yesterday and tomorrow in order to remain connected with You now.

Help me find peace in order that I may humbly try to define it when asked, as I know I will be. Your peace is what I want. Guide me only to seek this end, and then all else will follow as the natural order of things.

Thoughts on a Friend

Is it the spirit I love or the warmth of the smile?
Those incredible eyes—as deep and knowing as
Mother Earth—give love as they beckon you to enter
the soul.

This man who has chosen love as his path—what is
the lure, the connection, the level? Love enters the
room as he turns to greet me. Did he bring it or
is it my quest too? His embrace is so total it encompasses my being. It is not my body that feels
it, but my Inner Self basking in his light and love
and warmth. Is it the Christ consciousness I see? Yes,
maybe it is. And it lives in the body of this very
human being. His weaknesses and strengths make
him total and real, for one without the other denies
growth.

How can I give to this one who has so much? What
could I possibly add to the life of this man? At times,
I fear nothing; and yet, I choose to dissipate the
fear with lack of judgment and measurement. Let
me just ''be'' as I go forward. And, if there is but
one moment or thought, one inspiration or deed

that might affect his growth, then I am grateful beyond words.

There have been only a few moments together that
we have shared, yet much has transpired, some just
beyond comprehension.

Both his strength and gentleness draw me near and
I can finally understand why these opposites are so
compatible. It is surely true that only the very strong
could ever dare to be gentle.

I see the Light in this man I call friend and have
come to love every aspect of his being. May I always
be blessed with a lack of judgment and total acceptance of who he is at the moment. And as he changes,
may I always allow myself the needed room for
growth to accept and, hopefully understand what is
transpiring.

I trust in the Light for it will only lead me where I
am meant to go.

The Hermitage

I sat on the bench on the crest at the curve in the
road. The sun came to greet me and there I slept
and wept and read and meditated and I thought of
the ways that I love you. Each gave me peace.

Memories

When I remember New York I feel the warmth of the spring sun and the pulse of life aglow in the park.

When I remember New York I call forth again the sweet joy of your tears in the acceptance that a child that died was, and is, truly special.

When I remember New York I delight at the exuberance of a rising new Broadway star and wonder what Russian mother invented borsch for her young ones. I pray that somewhere on my path, I might lift the heart of a lonely piano player.

When I remember New York, I send a hug to a very beautiful tree who accepted our love with open branches amidst the sweet music of city angels.

When I remember New York I remember the peace in your eyes that you first brought into my room and my joy when you chose to have it remain. I remember your new found inner strength in choosing to love me and the gentleness with which it came to pass. I remember your touch and the tenderness I felt in the early morning hours as I watched you sleep. Your face was that of a child.

I remember dawn's light as my mind blended meditation with a half sleep. It transformed us to beings of light and intertwined and joined us far beyond any physical fantasies could imagine.

But, perhaps what I remember most of all from New York is that . . . I never will have to remember . . . for I learned those days that now is forever and all that was real will remain as part of today. The love and the caring, the sensitivities and the sharing —the vulnerability we both chose to feel. They are a part of us now . . . and it is we who are forever.

Spirit

Spirit, how I love Your Light. You are joy and beauty and everything right. You crystallize the evening sky as Your glow encompasses all that is.

You leave me now but only in presence. Your beams remain always to light my way from the darkened world home to You.

Spirit, cleanse me and purify my mind for it to fill only with thoughts of You. Time and space intertwine our illusions but You, Reality, guide us gently home.

Spirit, I yearn to keep You in my heart and as my mind moves to distraction, fill my entire being with Your Presence. You are the Light of my life and purpose of my existence.

Unafraid

I want to soar above the clouds and dance into their crests. I have always but skimmed the waters catching glances of reflections of the Light, the closest resemblance on this plane. But now, unafraid, I glide on high. I go beyond my land and custom and tradition. I open my heart to the differences in the world, deleting all judgments and comparisons. Now, I seek to make way freely to travel without the baggage of mental prejudice and distraction.

I want for nothing on this plane, save love, for nothing else has relevance. I am totally sustained by an act of giving and nothing is required in return.

For the first time, Spirit, I am no longer impatient to be back with You. You have calmed me and humbled me to a peace-filled plateau. From here I can function from Your Will. I feel Your immeasurable Love for me and it fills me beyond words.

I can only turn and give like, for it fills me to the brim.

You are the Way and the Light and I am a part of You; separate no more, alone no more. I will begin my final journey home to You with Your Presence encompassing my being.

You are. I am. We are one.

Prayer on Awakening

When you wake each morning, take all the love I have given to you and spread it as generously as you can on My gardens, never stopping to measure. Your cup will never run empty and I will fill it each night at the end of your journey far beyond the limits you first thought possible. You will nourish the flowers and tend the weeds and you, My gardener, will reap "wealth" beyond words.

The Flower Garden

Each morning the sun and moisture lit your crystal palace and it shimmered alive with your newly created patterns. The games we played, you and I, for oh so long—a daily ritual of removal and restoration. So determined were you; so confident of your patterns and pathways. I should have looked to you for the gifts of knowledge you offered in your natural daily doings, but, I only sought to rid my flowered garden of your persistence. In battle one day we fought head on. Your strength and spirit to hold firm on your journey forward stunned my being and the basest of my neurosis came forth to crush your hold on my beautiful flower bed. We fought and you fell under the torrent of water I directed at you—full force and you still held—web broken, lines torn free, and you still held—hanging from the last of your silver strands. The force was increased, and I, who had been long seeking to discover the culprit, successfully used my strength and that of the green tubular river to crush you. I have rid my flower garden of you for you have fallen to the ground far below. I have won! You invade my space no more.

Yet, why do I sit each morning now thinking of your silver, crystal web shimmering in the wind and miss my respect for your persistence and continuity —in awe when you reappeared each day in full construction. The memory of your final fall was filled with aggressiveness and confusion at the very nature of the battle.

I have won! I have rid you from my flower garden. Why do I ache so and mourn your loss? You were but a mere spider—clever and creative—yet, just a mere spider. There are millions of you. How have you amongst all become so much a part of my space when I felt you invaded my place? Perhaps, it is because the flower garden didn't belong to just me, and you were not a foreign invader claiming my treasures. Perhaps, just perhaps mind you, both you and I are part of the flower garden.

Possession was part of my neurotic amassment of "things" to barricade my space from the rest of the world—to keep you out. As I broke and destroyed your web the final time, I also broke down the walls of possessive junk. They have no value now that I have won the battle, for I was the one who sought to interrupt and change your destined journey. You have lost but a place and silver threads, yet, I have lost part of my soul. My strength and power were exercised in full during your invasion. I have lost the greatest of all. Yet, I have now gained from your example and the recognition of your right to live and to dwell in the flower garden as much as I.

I miss you fondly each morning as our friendly battle was most fun before I needed to conquer. Through losing you, may I remember the pain of conquest when the person rid the flower garden of the spider who only sought placement of a good view of the morning sun and a gentle breeze in the companionship of floral friends.

Let me hail your courage and creativity and let me hope to recognize again your Spirit in the next small creature I encounter, giving the respect deserved as we are equal in our rights to exist.

The flower garden was created for all . . .

Light

When the Light shines each day, discern not where the beams shall fall. Their directions are inherent in the nature of their being. Let them emit with no boundaries and they shall find their own directions.

The Venture

The time has come for me to venture forward. I am to make no claims to any objects or material goods. I will move forward without the burdens and distractions of material wares. In the simplicity of my life I will find peace and tranquillity.

No more will I be torn by the Source's will or mine. I will know confidence from deep in my heart, never again to fear any thought or thing. I will work to be a clear, crystal reflection of the Light—shining forth love in its purest form. I live in You always and we will travel together to the far corners of the earth. You have been there, so it will be no stranger to us.

The Web

Time will take hold of the days of my life and they will be spent searching for the Light now recognized on earth. I will help join the fragmented pieces of knowledge and form a web that will gradually encircle the earth. Its fibers will be woven from love and it will help support and sustain the future of humankind. The direction is mine, so I now go in peace to begin my work.

The Children

The children—they are the "resource" for love. Untouched and undeterred, they give it willingly and freely 'til shown otherwise. I will work to gather their many inspired thoughts on the Light, those thoughts inherent, not taught, and draw attention to the similarities. They are almost identical in their conception of the Source and they are the most correct of all the peoples. All will learn from the children, and so shall I. Many children will I come to know and love and embrace as my own. I have much love and can fill the needs, even when I think it not possible.

The Light is visible in many, but not so visible as in the children, the seeds in the garden. I will sow them and tend them and reap golden Light from their wisdom.

Direction

Today brings new insights as I begin to see. Clear vision begins to be mine as I am freed to venture forward.

The days will be long and full of love. Peace will be the basic component I will work with and the knowledge of the Whole, the Light, will emerge as seedlings from the ground. I will venture these days of my life filled with the knowledge that the Source is with me always.

Peace

Peace I've never known before; calm—the placid sea on a moonlit night. Confusion and distraction, activity and duty surround me. Yet, I am centered in a place I've never been before.

I have no questions, no doubts; no insecurities or fears remain. You asked for them, Spirit. I gave, and You have dispelled all of their illusions. You have left me filled with solid Light. There is no space open where love has not filled. I will carry Your gift of peace deep inside of me for the rest of my days here. I will carry it home to join again with You.

Listening

Following my heart, I listen to the sounds I hear there.

I want to search out and join the common fibers of the peoples of the planet. Join them in order that they might see their likenesses over their differences, their common goals over their disputes, their love over their hate. Their children are the connections. As I ask them, they will provide all the answers necessary to complete the image of the Light. Then, once known, all will learn from them.

Clear the way for the children to speak.

Patience

I am bound only by the borders of my mind and choose to open to the extensions of myself, the possible expansions beyond my now limited imagination.

As I grow my awareness will expand and love will broaden my mental, physical, and spiritual borders. I will have a clearer vision of what is true and I will function through that clarity.

I must be patient with the changes, and feel the love of the Source in me and around me all of the while. Being aware of Love's Presence, all will flow as naturally as the sea. I will soar into knowledge at a quickened rate of speed and love will balance the motion for me.

As I seek only peace, it will be mine.

Will

As I begin the day with Love's Presence on my mind, I allow it to reside in me and will come to feel the power there. It is the strongest of forces for it is the Universe's basic composition.

Love will come to guide each action of the day and enrich my moments with golden rewards.

Strength in the power of the Universe will flow through me when I am willing to accept the Will of the Source totally as my own. When this time has come, all else will wash away and the diluted illusions will be no more.

Soaring

Spirit, somewhere in Your sky I fly, downwind of change, soaring like an illusive wind. Change has no name; it encompasses all that is.

You are strength and confidence and gentleness in Your knowledge of the Light. You soar and observe, but do not search, for You are clear in Your vision of the Truth. I have yet to recognize fully my joyful part.

Come to the left and come to the right of me and raise me to where I will come to recognize the Source within. Help me find the reflection I so desperately need to free me of my self-delusions.

As I look at Love, let it reflect back to me for that is what I am.

As I look at the Light, let it reflect back to me for that is what I am.

And, as I look at Peace, let it reflect back to me for that is what I am.

You are—I am—we are One.

The Witness

If I could see You, Spirit, all of the while, I ask
myself then how would I act or think or be? Let
me begin to believe that You are always here, behind
my eyes and in the front of my mind. Let me live and
function in this life as if You were bearing witness to
every word, every breath, every endeavor . . . for
You are.

You and I

I need nothing from you. You are free to come and go in and out of my mind and my body.

I have no expectations of you; neither who you are or what you should be.

So, you are, therefore, bid freedom of metamorphosis from moment to moment and I will but indulge in the freeform of your figure.

You are not capable of disappointing me for in this act, comparison rules, and I compare you not. There is nothing to compare you with for as you were yesterday, you are gone today and a new you is being born again each moment in time.

Fear not my vision of you for it is only of the moment. It is clear and focused in love and total acceptance.

Mask yourself not, my friend of this flight, and journey with me beyond ourselves.

Confusion

Neither of us understand the Plan. Confusion abounds in this time of change. We should fear not, for Spirit is with us all the while. It will soon be clear to us both and we will begin to be. Distractions will fade and we will begin to see life's pattern for us.

We must not distort the insignificant happenings which now surround us. They are meant to cloud us in the world's eyes in order that the changes may all begin.

As we keep love close to our hearts and peace on our minds, we are not to take leave of each other as we must discover together strengths which lie within. We form a power far beyond our imaginings.

We are to love one another and the flood waters of our beings will begin to flow and move out over the earth.

The Discovery

We bring with us each day the Light and make its presence known. The Light is eternal and its continuity and guidance will open hearts to the new possibilities in love.

We are to journey today and each day of our stay with the Light in our hearts and eyes. Its presence in us will reflect beyond our wildest imaginings and it will give birth to its likeness in those who bear witness to our glow.

All will flow freely in bountiful joy when the heart is loosened and set free in flight. We will never know each day's directions until the moment of its birth, so love and trust in the Will, and our Inner Guidance will map our way along the journey.

Trust in the power and glory of the Presence and we will help carry the Lanterns of Light to guide the world home out of the darkness of fear into the day of Eternal Light.

Joy is abundant as we discover the Light, we

seekers of Truth. Fear will be gone forevermore as we trust our Inner Strength.

Beacons

Fill our hearts with the joy of love for all to see. Let others witness love as it could be. We both are capable of a relationship that bears the name of the Source, as yet unknown to the world around us. We come together and join our hearts with all for all.

Time will have it that the years will be brief. We will fill them each moment of the day with love unconditional borne from the Source. We will both rise above ourselves and join with the Light in holy relationship—one active, not passive, in the work.

Our wills will be a clear mirror of Divine Will and all acts will be done in the name of love, the name of Light, the name of the Source of all Creation.

As we join our minds, all else will flow. Our singleness of purpose, to be a living image of the Light, will touch the heart of the world. We will glow as a beacon of believability.

Beyond our comprehension is what we represent. But, we will take what is known to us and face the world. We will filter our love through each other, always cognizant of its singular Source.

Communion

Your twinkle—your smile, the very sun glistens from your radiant eyes when you caress me with your glance.

The child in a man's silhouette—innocence borne free from pain and experience. You have embraced the earth and her natural ways and she gives you forth her radiant glow.

Exuberant child of the Light—you touch the world and it touches you in return—Love flowing freely, an affair of the Spirit.

Come touch my heart and my lips and my soul—an interlude in the metamorphosis. Gentle child of the Light—I bid you welcome into my being. Your very presence on this plane helps light my way Home.

Come take my hand as we walk through time to a place where none exists—free from matter to fuse with the Light in communion forevermore.

Trust

Eye beyond eye, there is not vision enough on this planet to see the distance of one particle of Reality for it cannot be seen with the eyes nor heard with the ears nor created with the hands.

Of trust I am taught that it is only in the Source that true vision or voice or creativity is born. Beyond all corridors of the mind are the levels of comprehending it's strength. To be consciously joined with the Power in the Universe, I must delude my illusions of their very nature and presence. I will never channel the Source unless I delete my own for it is not real. Then, and only then, will I begin to truly experience the magnificence of the Presence within me.

I feel so close. It is but left to do. I will rise in the name of Creation and come forth into the world.

Love joins me with trust—a trust that spans beyond the planets and all matter. In my just "being," I represent that trust, a total vulnerability to the Will. I am on the border of this experience and am now beginning the journey inward beyond where I have ever gone before.

Trust in the Light for the Light is Trust.
Trust in Love for Love is Trust.
Trust in the Source for it is me and I am Trust.

Ego Recognition

My deluded illusions grab and clutch in a final desperate plea to give my ego recognition, but I am to fear not for it has none. As my "spring" arrives, I wrangle with the physical pain of unfolding. Yet, I know the peace and tranquility that lie before me—never again to be dormant.

My way is not an easy one, yet as the curtains of mist are cleared away, the Light becomes more visible to me and the pain of everyday living lessens. Fear not my rejection from him who walks by my side, for he rejects but my illusions and holds me close at heart. As I abide in Spirit, I will experience love and acceptance beyond my imaginings.

Testimony

Take the darkness from the hearts of the children. They are saddened by their aloneness, an illusive state which encompasses their reality. Beckon them to feel the Light living inside, a testimony to the Universal One of which they are a part. They do not conceive of their connection with all others and the isolation keeps them dormant to growth. We can be a testimony for the Light as we let it emit where it may to all whom we have thought or deed with. Our healing is a powerful source for their spirits and we are capable of loosening the bindings that hold their minds.

Look beyond ourselves, children of the Light, and allow the Presence to filter freely. Do not be afraid of what will result for it is in the name of Love that we will accomplish all. That alone, will make it plausible.

We are to toil not with daily occurrences, but finish them and let them pass. Time will soon free us of these, now that they are no longer necessary.

Love and trust and abide in the Light and all will flow with a continuity more familiar to us than we now realize. Joy will be abundant in our hearts and it will flow and carry all who experience our work to a higher level.

The time is here for Light. The dawn of Enlightenment is about to begin. Give praise to the Source and all of the children as they rise together in Light out of the chains of ignorance into the Womb of Love. The time for innocence has returned as the mandala begins its completion.

The Dedication

Eternal Light of our night, open our hearts and minds to hear Your words and wishes for us. Your will is all we seek in the name of peace. Teach us, Your seekers, to look to You each day of our stay for the way You wish us to be.

Guardian and Giver of Life, You are what is, and nothing else, save love, is real. I walk in You today and dedicate my being to Your Will and to spreading the Light.

Children of Light

Children of Light, beyond ourselves will we travel to the borders of time. We will carry the Light deep in our hearts and leave a connection with the Source on each particle of soil we touch, with each soul we encounter.

Behold the magnificence of people so very different, and yet, the same. They all toil with life's survival and hope that a Higher Power exists to save the sanity of the planet. They feel all is beyond their control, yet they can come to learn that peace and hope and love are at the foundation inside each of them. Fear them not the warriors of our time, for the ultimate peace will arise from each individual being when they commune with the Source of all life.

We are messengers, couriers of the news. Mother Father God is alive and loving and oversees all that is and was and will be.

We will let them know that all will be supported and guided who choose the way of love and peace. It can be accomplished, peace on this plane. And, in time, it will. But, all must join their part with the Whole in the way that is familiar and appropriate for them.

The Source goes with us as we travel to touch the heart of the world on our journey in Light.

Transcendence

Above all else, love will carry the world from darkness into Light, from ignorance into knowledge, from bondage into freedom.

Another plateau are we about to enter. We will neither decipher nor expect what we believe the plans may be; only accept the love as it flows through us.

As we have transcended pain, it means not that there will be none; as we have transcended vanity, clothe ourselves we must still, yet without the preoccupation of such. Each earthbound description of us has been transcended and the last and most difficult has just transpired. The pleasures of the body we have set aside to fill our minds with the Light. Yet, loving still we must, and sharing the emotion we will for denial serves not. It is only in the achievement of balance, the accomplishment of harmony, that all earthbound descriptions find their place. The lack of dominance of any free us to function in the natural, free flowing state we were born into.

Each moment will be filled with love and Light and the knowledge of the Whole. Free ourselves to "just be" and our love of the Source and each other will illuminate the road homeward for the world to see.

Live, love and be at peace.

The Illusion of Time

As the illusion of time

is finally laid to rest,

the Reality of the Love

that eternally binds us

all together as One

comes forth

and our separateness from

God is no more.

Heaven and earth are joined

and our One, true Self

emerges to lighten the world.

Infant Child

Infant Child . . . In your eyes is love born forever free as it disregards race and national ties as if they did not exist. Infant Child . . . You are the hope of the world and it is in your image and likeness that I find my task for transformation. You are joy-filled in your very existence, and you trust as a part of the natural flow.

Unconditionally loving, you are connected without exception to all those around you. The touch of the flower and your mother's embrace are equally pleasurable to your unbiased senses.

Infant Child . . . I search back before I shut you out. I closed myself to you as early as I could in order to sophisticate my adolescence. I now wander in a nameless, homeless state as I search in the dark corridors of egoism. You are my key to identity. Call my name once again, Infant Child. Call to me . . ''Love'' . . for that is who we are, you and I, one in the same.

As I search you out you will find your way home, orphaned one. Call to me clearly once again for this time I will listen for you. It is the hour for us to join again, you and I as we, to dwell in the Spirit of our heart. We are joined forevermore and known by our long forgotten name, Love.

Letting Go

Be kind of heart and let the lessons flow, for these are the fruits of labor. It is in these lessons that all will be learned to pave the way Home. Time is an illusion and all can be accomplished in an instant, but the experience of choice must be applied to each plateau.

I will trust my Inner Guidance to go forth on this journey. As I let all be, I learn of the peace that living in the now proclaims.

As I let go of the boundaries, the expectations, the self-serving directions, I am freed.

Gift of Life

Look to the east and look to the west and to all points north and south and nowhere will you find peace but inside of the heart of your own being.

Trust that the rays of sun which connect all life will hold you safely in your gentle cocoon of chrysalis.

Emerge into Light as radiant and pure as the rays you embrace, for in your visibility lies a reflection as with all others who seek the Source.

Seek and you shall find. Hold no expectations and all will be yours.

Delete the need to understand anything and all knowledge will flow through you.

Be gentle of heart and you will be empowered with ultimate strength.

Be joyful and dance to the music of life lightening the loads of those dwelling in shadows.

Sing praise to the simplicity of the natural way by the very essence of your being.

Give praise to the Light and happiness and joy—filled days will abound.

Be kind as all remnants of anger and fear dissipate into dust.

Be light of heart as you dwell in the place of angels with each moment of laughter.

Drink of the beauty of life as its abundance gives you complete fulfillment.

Love as your gift of life and transcend to Light on this the border of the death of time.

Spirit Within

Spirit within, I reach for the sun to touch your Source. Beyond all doubts lies your presence within. I intertwine in consciousness with You, particle upon particle of knowledge and intuitive knowing. I search for the connection in Oneness and find peace in the harmony of the flow.

Sisters and Brothers in Light, we search the dark corridors of the mind for Your answers, only to find their refuge in our hearts, the towers of all knowingness.

Beyond each day's struggle lies the Infinite Power within, the totalness of "being," the reality of peace. Guide us to the threshold of love, the opening to pure consciousness of Light. It is so familiar, and now just within reach.

Touch the World

Touch the world from the place centered in the heart and remain the selfless bearer of truth.

Beckon not self-serving illusions to fill the void of time and space, but reach to the core to produce a reality of the one vision of hope.

Come to the world with an openness of heart and lay to rest the falsehood of desire, the fear of wanting, and the futility of pursuit.

Live in Spirit's Will and all will be fulfilled through the pure power of Creation. All will be beyond your imaginings.

Claim the Light that is yours to bear and carry the lantern of love into the darkened world of illusions.

Perceive not Spirit's plan, but go in the joy of the now. All will come to pass in perfect harmony if you but believe it is so.

Go in the peace that the moment is now. Go in love, for that is what you are.

PART THREE

The Journey Home

Destiny

Reach for your destiny for it is you who weaves the carpet upon which you walk. It is your choice of fiber and texture, durability as well as brilliance. Only you can decide upon your future and the decision to no longer decide is where your destiny truly awaits you.

Come into the Light and feel the richness of its glow. The Golden Rays are all about you in those you have come to recognize as familiar. Join with them to light up the world for the new dawn of the age of enlightenment.

Feel the way of your intuitive Force and follow your call.

Desire

At this moment in time there is nothing that I have ever wanted or needed that I now desire that is not of the Spirit. Reality encompasses all.

Peace and love. Nothing else exists. All else is illusion. As I transform from the dream to reality, this becomes clear as the Crystal Light.

I want nothing.

I need nothing.

There is no longer desire for what is lacking. The Source provides for me always all that which is necessary for complete happiness. I need but to love myself enough to accept the totalness of just being in the Light.

I accept this moment as one totally complete for I am joined with that which is completeness.

I accept this moment as being totally loved for I am joined with Spirit who is love.

I accept the Peace of this moment as the final goal fulfilled for I am at one with all and the illusive barriers of time and space are void.

A Friend's Marriage

The hour is near for you to take vows with another, he whom you have chosen as your fellow seeker of Truth. You cross my mind and therefore, you touch my heart and affect my journey. To observe a conscious joining of spirits in human form solicits thoughts of potential and visions of skies of great expanse.

We question relationships "special," since all persons should be experienced with maximum possibilities in love. Yet, does not each person we encounter nourish a separate root? Are we not fragmented in our potential growth and, thus, influenced unequally from each source we encounter?

If there is one who can, therefore, nurture and bring forth from us our greatest and most beautiful blossoms, then are we not to allow ourselves to accept this with loving kindness for ourselves as we excite in the potential for mutual growth?

On the eve of the hour of your joining with another, I pray for your courage in accepting with maximum momentum the fullest joys and emotions you can experience as you journey into each other, thereby allowing the glow of your happiness to reach out and touch the rest of us, so in need of experiencing joy and love without guilt and reservations.

Gibran has said that "Love is the only freedom in the world because it so elevates the spirit that the laws of humanity and the phenomena of nature do not alter its course."

I wish for you, above all other gifts, the freedom and courage to love.

I wish it for you, and I wish it for me, and I wish it for all of us children.

Peace.

Fulfilled

I awoke in the morning, my love, conscious of your presence on the planet.

My awareness of Spirit is keen these days—Divine Will and peace my single goal.

You intertwine in the possibilities of the achievement of these. Yet, no future foretelling is real for only the moment will truly dictate my path Home.

Illusions come and go . . . shall I leave you forever and nevermore to meet?

But, would you really leave my mental world or would I harbor and give you sanctuary there?

My wanting you goes so far beyond physical presence as the mist momentarily rises.

Sometimes, as now, I am perfectly fulfilled knowing you are of the Light—sharing its glow somewhere at distance that does not exist.

At this moment we are totally joined in a timeless, placeless, communion of the Spirit and I am at peace.

Questions

On the crest high above the hills the early morning sun's reflection blinded me until my vision accepted only its shimmering crystal light and no other view.

I asked Spirit to dispel my illusions—to sever my wants—to expose my desires. "Lay me, Spirit, into the humblest of roles so I may see Your way for me." It is not knowing that leads me to distraction. If I could but know, then I would follow.

I asked as I turned to walk down the knoll, "How shall I love above longings and desires, wantings and fulfillments?"

Light touched my shoulder and turned me into the warmth of the sun's embrace as I heard from inside, "Say unto him who lives in your heart 'I love you as a child, for I had to become like a child to love you.'"

And so, the tumultuous waters in me became calm and I was at peace for I recognized in the love of a child total trust, an easy giving of the heart, exuberant joy in the opportunity for life, and, therefore, I recognized . . . love.

A Microcosm

You thank me for my patience, yet it is not patience I have for you, it is love.

Patience has no place in my feelings for you for it is a result of judgment that you are not where you should be. My love for you fills me with the knowledge that you are exactly where you should be at this moment in time and that it is all perfect just the way it is.

Love has no levels. It is but our acceptance of it that changes and fluctuates. As we experience these transitions we begin to comprehend the boundless and everlasting Source of which we are a part.

Our relationship is not a substitute for what could be; it is but a limited part of what is. It is a microcosm of potential growth for all relationships. Look beyond your fears, my loving friend, and have faith that Spirit would never lead you where It's strength cannot keep you.

The Hour

Spirit, You have granted me love from every direction here; and as I entered this journey, You gifted me with the innate knowledge that You'll love me beyond my forever no matter how much I falter. You direct me that now is the hour to set my love free . . . love born unconditionally from Your part . . . to flow as the river of life through the veins of all I encounter.

You ask this of me not in question for whether I am capable, but rather that it is who I am. I am Your Heart and Your Spirit. You are the life unto me, beyond the breaths I take and the vibrations my heart beats.

You are life itself and joy unto us who recognize Your Presence equally in a blade of grass and in a struggling soul.

Remembering

Spirit, You asked me to take but a few moments in time to share with my sisters and brothers Your Light. I left my wings and my ability to fly to be grounded here for those moments for which we agreed.

At times I am angry, as I stand on the hillside and cannot take flight. It is because for the moment I have forgotten with how much love You asked me to come. I have forgotten Your small request in my consumption with the frustration and weight of my human form.

Transcendence lies far beyond humility and I chose to be here to teach and to learn. Help me to remember my humanness as a gift from You in the opportunity to further understand myself and my Source.

Far beyond me is the nature of the boundlessness of Your Love and it is only when I remember my part of that Whole that I become calm again in the peace of Your Presence.

The Purpose

We are children of the Light, never again to be lost or to feel deserted. Our existence will be singular in purpose. We are to give love, to extend it everywhere and at all times. We will help define the word "unconditional" and in doing so, the Presence will be experienced further.

We will now go beyond ourselves to dwell and connect in full consciousness with all that is. Love will flow with a current strong enough to move the heart of the world. We have no fear left, and it is from this point that we will depart.

Clouded Layers

Beneath the clouded layers of each day's tasks lies the function and purpose of the Source. It will be shown in its time. I have not been fearful that the way is unclear for the light of the darkened rooms of my mind has been the source of my vision. All will be clear in time.

Peace on my mind and the Presence in my heart is all I need do. Be quiet. Be at Peace. Trust that all is as it should be.

Perceived Loss

The floodwaters of confusion rush forward and envelop me. I fear not the loss of perspective for some aspects must be left behind as my view changes. The broadening of my way into the world will result in tremendous change; change born of weighted debris being lifted from me forever.

I make my way in peace for in doing so I pave the road for some others. It is the Source who will give me direction. I am never to fear that the Light does not dwell within me for It will give me the vision necessary to see my way Home.

I will be quiet at this time and go inward to find Spirit dwelling there.

The Road

If I have learned of specialness

and if I have learned detachment

and if joy in the Divine Will

is finally my only goal,

Am I so far off course?

Separateness

As the illusion of time

is finally laid to rest,

the reality of the love

that eternally binds us

all together as One

comes forth

and our separateness from

the Source is no more.

Heaven and earth are joined

and our One, true Self

emerges to lighten the world.

Spirit Within

Spirit within I reach for the sun to touch Your Source. Beyond all doubts lies Your Presence within. I intertwine in consciousness with you, particle upon particle of knowledge and intuitive knowing. I search for the connection in oneness and find peace in the harmony of the flow.

Brothers and Sisters in Light, we search the dark corridors of the mind for our answers, only to find their refuge in our hearts, the towers of all-knowingness.

Beyond each day's struggles lies the Infinite Power within, the totalness of being, the reality of peace. Guide us to the threshold of love, the opening to pure consciousness of Light.

Releasing

I need not hold myself to unjust expectations of what my role is to be, with whom, or why. I will be positioned in the world exactly as it should be if I but release my ties to past and future and to those close in my arena.

My expectations stop the process and interrupt the flow. I indeed know the purpose of my life for I have been prepared for this. But, most importantly is the way of life—the means to the end of this journey. I need do nothing if I stay attuned to the Spirit within.

The attachments must be released to all persons and things before I can flow with the Source in the true tide of my life. I must watch each day to avoid the traps of the ego. Hold on to no one and I will be separate from none. As I free all others, I free myself in the process.

I need solitude and a path of my own to walk on each day as I end this phase and begin the final journey out into the world. I need the time and space now in order to complete this in the manner that it needs to be done. It seems complex and I hold on and tend to avoid movement, but it is the holding on that is stopping the flow for I block the energy needed from within to make it happen. I myself block it with internal barriers to my truth.

It is only a matter of time before it all flows. As I acknowledge the Source in this moment, it will all begin. It is my choice and mine alone for all has been provided for me to accomplish the work I came here to do. I choose the Light because there is for me ultimately no other choice.

The Combination

Sometimes we rise above and sometimes we fall below.

Sometimes we leap for joy and sometimes we wrench with pain.

But always we go forward and always we continue for the journey is such that it is a combination of all.

I touch you, my beloved brothers and sisters, as I touch each of these experiences for we have chosen the journey together, and I am forever eternally grateful for our choice.

Come, let us continue homeward.

Exploration

Beyond the boundaries of the unlighted mind there is a consciousness wherein lies a new perception of love and clarity of all that it is not. As I delve inside to find the passageway to this consciousness, I find the avenue where no judgments exist nor measurements function.

Beyond my self-imposed limitations lies the answers. As I delete judgment, delete measurement, and delete the need to understand, I will clear the space for love to flourish and grow.

Exploring this realm is my path. I explore it in peace, explore it in joy, and explore it as part of all that I am.

I go in peace and the knowledge that all will unfold as it should. All questions will find resolution as their meaninglessness is exposed. All love will be experienced and received when it is set free.

Humility

Humble me to a place on the planet, Spirit, where I might dwell in gentleness while functioning from Your Strength. Remind me that my actions are not only labels for what I believe in, but expressions of Your Love.

Expand my awareness to encompass the most delicate of organisms, the most forgotten extensions of my being that soar in the air and dwell in the sun baked crevasses of the earth. Particle on particle, we are all molecules of the same nucleus. I will find completeness as I recognize and join in celebrating my oneness with all that is on this plane.

Joined in oneness, I celebrate Your Life unto me. I am You and, separate from this, is nothing.

Spirit within, move me to join with all that I am in full consciousness in order to join with You.

It is the hour of oneness. Separation, the illusion, is no more.

The Gift of Self

I recognize my journey as a call to honor the Spirit within, the Source of all life. In order to respond to this call I must first come to honor the human being that is me. In denying or blocking my gifts or my growth, I deny the tools of the Creator who allowed me to bring them into this life. Since they are part of me who is in turn part of all that is, I do honor to the Source of Creation by manifesting all that I am capable of being. For this new awareness, I am humbly grateful for I realize that the greatest gift of love I can give is the fullest expression of the gift of self.

NOTES

NOTES

NOTES

NOTES

NOTES

NOTES

NOTES

NOTES

NOTES

NOTES